THE POWER OF APPROACHABILITY

How to Become an Effective, Engaging Communicator One Conversation at a Time

By Scott Ginsberg
©2005 Front Porch Productions

THE POWER OF APPROACHABILITY

Scott Ginsberg
Copyright © 2005 Front Porch Productions

Printed in the United States of America.

Cover design and text layout by Jeff Braun at
TriFecta Creative, St. Louis, Missouri
www.trifectacreative.com

ISBN: 0-9726497-1-9

What People Are Saying About The Power of Approachability...

"The world would be a better place if more people would adopt Scott's straightforward approach to communication."
Catherine Ryan Hyde, Author of Pay it Forward, Electric God and Walter's Purple Heart

---

"Scott offers specific, practical, and easy ways we can all become more approachable, whether in business or in friendship. Any organizational leader who want to help their members work together more effectively and enjoyably should read this."
Susan J. Ellis, President, Energize, Inc.

"Concise and powerful and techniques applicable to any generation wanting to make a more powerful personal and professional connection ... a must read and a must have resource on your shelf!"
Dr. Jeff Magee, PDM, CSP, CMC, Publisher/PERFORMANCE Magazine, CEO of JEFF MAGEE INTERNATIONAL

"Scott is quickly becoming the authority on approachability. His book is a powerful learning tool, entertaining and a delight to read. It is a must for all professionals – young and old – who want to master their interpersonal potential."
Andy Masters, Author, Life After College: What to Expect and How to Succeed in Your Career

---

"If you want to become more approachable and improve your networking skills in a matter of hours, not days, put this book at the top of your must-read list. Scott has created a one-of-a-kind, how-to-BECOME guide that can help all of us leverage every interaction."
Ron Ameln, Editor, St. Louis Small Business Monthly

"I love Scott's stuff. And unlike so many other business books, this one is fun to read! More importantly, it is filled with common sense information that is easy to put into action and contribute to your success in life and business."
Shep Hyken, Author, The Loyal Customer and Moments of Magic

"Scott's conversational tone combined with concrete, practical advice offers solid solutions for anyone that needs to communicate more effectively."
Todd Brockdorf, President, Brockdorf Productions

ABOUT THE AUTHOR

Scott Ginsberg is the author of two books including *HELLO, my name is Scott and The Power of Approachability*. In addition to writing dozens of articles for various publications each year, Scott is also a member of the National Speaker's Association and frequently speaks to colleges, businesses and organizations around the country who want to become more effective, engaging communicators - one conversation at a time. Some of his clients include The Boeing Company, Coldwell Banker Gundaker, University of Las Vegas Nevada, Missouri Meetings and Events, The United Methodist Church of the Shepherd and the National Council for Marketing and Public Relations.

Scott has been wearing a nametag all day, every day since November 2, 2000 for the sole purpose of increasing approachability. He has been internationally recognized as the **world's foremost field expert on nametags** by the *Washington Post*, CNN, The Associated Press, Headline News, *USA Today* and dozens of other media outlets.

For booking or more information, please contact:

Front Porch Productions
PO Box 410684
St. Louis, MO 63141
www.hellomynameisscott.com
scott@hellomynameisscott.com

ACKNOWLEDGMENTS

This book would not exist without the following people:

My loving and supportive parents, because of whom I have no reason to complain about anything.

My entire family, the greatest family ever.

William Jenkins, a man who serves as my mentor, teacher, preacher, coach, inspiration and best friend.

Shep Hyken, who shows me the ropes.

Chad Kouse of Aheadhosting, my good friend and amazing web designer.

Kirk Lintern, my good friend from Cheyenne Arapaho who's always on my back to post more stories.

My editors, who saw the things I didn't: Andy Masters, Adam Erwin, Cheri Hanstien, Ron Ameln, Adrianne Mikosz, Todd Brockdorf, Dr. Jeff Magee, Shep Hyken, Paul Wesslemann, Allison Rockamann, William Jenkins, Susan Ellis and Aaron Margolis.

Chuck Downs of Hey Doodle Doodle Studios, whose cartoons always make me laugh out loud.

Jeff Braun of TriFecta Creative, for his beautiful design and layout work.

Ron Ameln and the St. Louis Small Business Monthly, who support and run my articles.

Phoenix Photography, for their efficient photo production.

Steven Pressfield, author of *The War of Art*, my favorite book.

Dave Barry, the funniest man alive and my favorite writer.

Kate Miller, who told me to stop planning and just write.

Janet Kelley of MACO, who gives me LOTS of nametags.

Anyone who ever wrote me hate mail, because I always need a good laugh.

Otis and Ginger, my two favorite coworkers.

For Garrett, the stranger on the bus who changed my life.

TABLE OF CONTENTS

GINSBERG'S GLOSSARY

If the world had a front porch like we did back then
we'd still have our problems but we'd all be friends.
Treating your neighbor like he's your next of kin
wouldn't be gone like the wind.
If the world had a front porch, like we did back then.

TRACEY LAWRENCE, *IF THE WORLD HAD A FRONT PORCH*

INTRODUCTION

I KNEW IT WAS A CRAZY IDEA ... BUT I DIDN'T KNOW IT WOULD CHANGE everything.

That was my thought over four years ago when this book was born. I was in college at the time. And one night, I made a choice to do something a little different. Something nobody expected. Something fun!

I began to make *small changes* to the way I interacted with people. I literally *threw myself out there* to become more open, accessible and available to those around me. And as a result, I walked away from conversations *knowing* that my attitudes and actions made others feel appreciated, comfortable and welcomed.

In other words, I experienced the **power of approachability.**

The term *approachability* is not a characteristic. It's not a personality trait. Approachability is a way of life. It is a way of business, a way of conversation and a way of social interaction. It is the key to becoming an effective, engaging communicator – one conversation at a time. And *that* is what gives it so much power.

WHAT YOU WILL LEARN IN THIS BOOK

Approachability is a **two way street:** you must *approach* others, and, you must *be approachable* to others. So, because approachability is a function of many facets, what you are about to read is not just a how-to-be book. It's a how-to-**BECOME** book:

- How to **BECOME** a great conversationalist
- How to **BECOME** UNFORGETTABLE™ in your first impressions
- How to **BECOME** a Networking Superhero
- How to **BECOME** the epitome of approachability

In short: how to **BECOME** an effective, engaging communicator – one conversation at a time.

You will learn how to apply the power of approachability to several contexts of your life including personal, conversational, business, organizational and even technological. For that reason, it's important to first examine this word's various meanings to which I will allude throughout the book.

The word **approachability** has a diverse etymological history. It originally derives from the Latin adjective *propinquus,* or "neighboring."

However, the more common connection is to the Latin verb *appropiare*, or "to go nearer to.*"* So, because it would be difficult to pin down just *one* meaning on such a powerful word, you are going to learn how to take the term to the next level. Based on thousands of hours of reading, writing, research and experience, I have developed **The Six Power Principles** of the term *approachability*:

1. *Ready to engage*

2. *Accessible and easy to deal with*

3. *Available to others*

4. *Friendly and ready to listen and help*

5. *Easy to meet, converse or do business with*

6. *Capability of being reached*

Throughout this book, each chapter will elaborate on one of these **Power Principles**. Now, no one of these definitions is better than the others – just more applicable depending on the person and the situation. Also, to take those Power Principles a step further, each chapter will pose several thought provoking, application-driven questions called "Let Me Ask Ya This…" These questions will help you put to practice many of the new ideas in the book.

WHY I WROTE THIS BOOK

Every year I read and research hundreds of books, articles, websites, journals and multimedia resources about the social-psychology of human interaction, conversation, networking, first impressions and other topics related to interpersonal communication. However most of these resources only dedicate between a paragraph and a page to "being approachable." They never tell you **why** or, more importantly, **how** to be approachable. They just tell you to do it. They only scratch the surface. And that's a shame.

I wrote this book to offer a new paradigm to an old idea, and here it is: **basic to all victory in interpersonal communication is how** *approachable* – **and how *willing to approach others* – you are**. Yes, it suggests a different way of looking at communication. Yes, it requires a heightened appreciation for your conversational routines. But while taking the time to reexamine your daily encounters may seem mundane, it's difficult to become an effective, engaging communicator if you don't learn how to *throw yourself out there*. So, as you read this book, prepare yourself to look at every interaction – business, personal or otherwise – from this simple perspective:

Approachability is a way of life.
Become the epitome of it.

CHAPTER ONE

HELLO, my name is Scott

Throw Yourself into the Sea

"If you want to plant for days, plant flowers;
if you want to plant for years, plant trees;
and if you want to plan for life, plant ideas."

OG MANDINO

SO THERE I WAS – SITTING IN THE AUDIENCE OF AN ON-CAMPUS SEMINAR. Surrounding me sat hundreds of my fellow Miami University students; each of us wearing one of those little, handwritten, adhesive nametags.

When the event was over, we all filed toward the exit. I approached the door and noticed a small trashcan filled to the brim with ripped up, used nametags.

And that gave me an idea. A crazy idea. Maybe I should keep my nametag on all night!

I wondered what would happen if I "threw myself out there." And I wondered how that would affect my approachability.

Sure enough, I walked out of that seminar with "Scott" stuck on my chest. It looked a little something like this:

About 10 minutes later I met up with a friend of mine at a local ice cream shop. And that's when it all started. That's when the silence was broken.

People began to say hello. Random students walked up to me and started conversations. Even complete strangers yelled "Hey Scott!" from across the room! I noticed an astonishing increase in both *my own* and *other people's* willingness to communicate – all because of a nametag!

In other words, all because of **approachability.**

Later that night I returned home. I looked in the mirror at that little red and white nametag. And then, I made *the* most important decision of my entire life:

I vow to wear this nametag all day, every day – for the rest of my life.

That fateful day was November 2nd, 2000. And since then, my entire life has changed. On January 1st, 2003, my first book entitled *HELLO, my name is Scott: Wearing Nametags for a Friendlier Society*, was released. That book chronicled my adventures in nametagging through stories, experiments and anecdotes – and it painted a picture of approachability.

But with every passing day of wearing a nametag – I was forced to look deeper. I knew there was something bigger at work. And now after more than four years of wearing a nametag all day, every day – it's time to go from **experimental** to **experiential.**

In the midst of the thousands of hellos, encounters, conversations and interactions initiated by my nametag – one facet of approachability was most common: engagement. That's the first lesson in this book:

POWER PRINCIPLE #1
BEING APPROACHABLE MEANS BEING READY TO ENGAGE

Most interpersonal communication texts state that humans engage with each other for the following reasons:

THE MOTIVATORS OF HUMAN ENGAGEMENT
- *To help* – console, minister to the needs of others
- *To learn* – acquire info about others, themselves and the world
- *To relate* – establish and maintain interpersonal relationships
- *To influence* – control, manipulate, direct
- *To play* – enjoy themselves, escape from work

After I examined my field research and observations carefully, I looked for trends among the reactions. As a result, I discovered the direct correlation between the above motivators of human engagement and wearing a nametag all the time.

My data were organized into a system called "The Big Five Personality Types": ***The Inquirer, The Player, The Joker, The Customer, The Hero***

In this chapter, we'll examine each of "The Big Five Personality Types," all of which are categorized by a percentage. This percentage will show you the frequency with which each specific nametag encounter occurs on a daily basis – in proportion to all of the nametag encounters that occur on a daily basis. As you read through them, reflect not only on the humor and intrigue of the interactions; but also on each category's connection to a specific facet of approachability.

PERSONALITY TYPE #1: THE INQUIRER – 35%

In over four years, the most common reaction to my nametag has always been one of the following questions:

- Why are you wearing a nametag?

- What's the deal with the nametag?

- Where did you come from that you still need a nametag?

- What convention were you at?

- Did you have a meeting tonight?

- Where do you work?

People ask these questions to satisfy their curiosity. They just *have* to know. Nametags are traditionally worn for businesses, conventions, meetings and the like. So, it's natural for strangers who see me wearing one – at 11:00 PM on a Tuesday night at the gas station, for example – to ask why. In other words, they want to acquire information about others, i.e., **Engagement Motivator #2:** *to learn.*

As I detailed in my first book, *HELLO, my name is Scott*, my response to this type of inquiry is the "Skin and Bones" answer:

> *"I always wear a nametag – it encourages people*
> *to be friendlier and more approachable."*

That's what I say every time. Sometimes people smile. Sometimes people tilt their heads and nod in agreement. Sometimes people follow up with another question. Or, sometimes people look at me strangely, utter "Oh-kaaay," and walk away!

The key is: **they always engage** – with a complete stranger, nonetheless. It's happened to me in stores, at the gym, on the street, at restaurants, on the bus, in the elevator, walking down the hall, riding on escalators, even in the *bathroom*. Name a place – and I'm sure someone used my nametag to engage with me there!

I always found this facet of approachability (starting conversations) to be vital to communication success. Especially with new people, it can be difficult. Psychologically, people are afraid to do so because of a fear of rejection. And often times, they just don't know what to say (Chapter 5 will explore this in more detail).

But because of *The Inquirer*, the silence was broken. The interaction began. And an encounter – that otherwise would not have existed – initiated simply because of my nametag. This was my first lesson in approachability: **people engage with those who pique their curiosity.**

Let me ask you this...

How could you encourage people to break the silence with you?

PERSONALITY TYPE #2: THE PLAYER – 30%

I'll never forget my lunch with Carol and Susan. We went out to a restaurant in downtown St. Louis after attending a seminar on volunteerism. Afterwards, I decided to walk them to the nearby movie theater even though I was unable to stick around for the film. As we approached, I noticed the manager was ripping tickets at the entrance. That was my cue to say goodbye.

"Thanks for lunch Susan! It was great to see you today," I said, followed by a big, friendly hug.

"And Carol – it's always good to see you too. I'll email you next week about those cartoons we talked about," I said while I gave her an equally big, friendly hug.

The manager, having watched this show of friendship and spying on my nametag, ripped their tickets. And before Susan and Carol took a step into the theater, he opened his arms wide, walked up to me and said, "Scott...it was great to see you today! How about a hug?!" We all burst into laughter! And without a hitch, I gave the manager a huge hug.

I've been wearing a nametag for over four years – and that has NEVER happened before. I must say, it was one of the friendliest moments I ever experienced. And all the manager did was take advantage of the free offering of my name.

As Dale Carnegie[1] noted over 50 years ago, "A person's own name is the sweetest sound he will hear in any language." For example, think about when *you* go out to eat, shop at retail stores or attend meetings and conventions. Don't you use the names of complete strangers simply because they're wearing nametags?

Of course you do! Everyone does!

So, because most people understand the value of names – this type of interaction happens to me daily. That's why this personality type is called *The Player*. This person uses my name simply because he or she *can*.

- Hey *Scott*!

- Excuse me, *Scott.*

- Can I help you *Scott?*

- Here's your grande coffee, *Scott.*

Players use this "test the waters" approach to see whether I will:

a) Say hello back to them

b) Freak out and wonder how the heck they knew my name

c) Ignore them completely

(The correct answer is "a")

Anytime *The Players* use my nametag as a reference point or conversation starter, they're simply trying to establish the connection. Therefore, *The Player* personality type represents **Engagement Motivator #3:** *to relate.* It establishes and maintains interpersonal relationships. So, *The Player* taught me another lesson in approachability: **names are the most powerful tool for getting off to on the right foot with someone new.**

Names ➞ Self-Disclosure ➞ Rapport ➞ Trust

Let me ask you this...

Do you identify and amplify people's names to make them feel appreciated and connected to you?

PERSONALITY TYPE #3: THE JOKER – 20%

When I was living in Portland, Oregon a few years ago, I had an upstairs neighbor named Dave. The first time I met him, he asked about my nametag. I of course, offered him my standard response. Then, at the end of the conversation he joked, "Well *Jeff*, it was nice to meet you. I'll be seeing ya!"

This brings me to another frequently asked question, "Scott – do people ever make fun of you for wearing a nametag all the time?"

Perhaps a better question would be, "Scott – how *often* do people make fun of you for wearing a nametag all the time?"

Three to five times a day.

But have you ever heard the phrase, "Everyone's a comedian"? Well, according to my research, only about 20% of the people are comedians. Here are the most common one-liners from *The Joker* in response to my nametag:

- You must be Scott…

- Is your name Scott?

- I bet that's Scott over there![2]

- Do you have a memory problem or something?

- Is that so you don't forget your name?

- *What's* your name again?

- Do you wear your nametag in case you get lost?

- Did you just come from an A.A. meeting?

In spite of my embarrassment – and sometimes downright humiliation – I still consider encounters with *The Joker* to be positive. As these interactions show, *The Joker* still engages in conversation, even if he's making fun of me. *The Joker* still extends himself – often times to a complete stranger – in a light hearted, comfortable way. Hey, it's fun! What's more, *The Joker* enjoys himself, i.e., **Engagement Motivator #5** – to *play*. This is a surefire way to lighten up the encounter for both parties!

There's a valuable lesson to be learned from *The Joker*: **humor disarms people, especially complete strangers**. It changes the entire dynamic of the conversation when introduced in a fun, polite manner. As a matter of fact, many friends of mine are former strangers who noticed my nametag, approached me and started joking around!

Let me ask you this...

Can you think of someone who had you laughing the moment you met her?

PERSONALITY TYPE # 4: THE CUSTOMER – 10%

It's common to see people wearing nametags at meetings, events, churches, conventions, seminars and the like. But the one group of people most commonly identified with wearing nametags is: employees.

Wal-Mart was the first business to require all its employees to wear nametags. Sam Walton created this initiative because he wanted his customers to "get to know the people they bought from." This makes sense. After all, if customers need assistance in a store, restaurant, club or any other place of business – whom do you think they'll ask for help?

That's right – **the guy wearing the nametag**.

I was strolling through the aisles of Office Depot once when an elderly lady with a walker approached me, looked at my nametag and asked, "Excuse me Scott, can you tell me where the envelopes are?"

My face turned to stone. I paused for a split second, looked around and noticed an envelope end cap on Aisle 19.

Oh hell, why not.

I then said, "Yes Ma'am they're right this way..." as I escorted her down the aisle!

We made our way over to the rack. I crouched down to explore her mailing options and said, "Well...it appears there are...uh...5 X 8's, 8 X 10's...and...oh look! There's a sale on some padded envelopes for all of your packing and shipping needs!

"Oh thank you Scott – that's exactly what I needed."

And I said, "No Ma'am, thank YOU – for shopping at Office Depot!"

This wasn't the first, the last or the only time someone made the assumption that my nametag automatically denoted employment. It's a perfectly logical assumption. After all, who in their right mind would walk around wearing a nametag all the time?!

Just kidding. But over the years, I've been asked many questions about many products at many businesses. That's why the fourth personality type is called *The Customer*. Here's a short list of some of the jobs I've (falsely) held and places I've (falsely) worked:

Clothing Salesman	*Office Depot Customer Service Agent*
Produce Sanitizer	
Kinko's Project Manager	*Fondue Maitre D*
High School Teacher	*Karate Instructor*
Junior High School Teacher	*Personal Fitness Trainer*
Sunday School Teacher	*Computer Lab Technician*
Underwear Stock Boy	*Hardware Store Clerk*
Coat Checker	*COMP USA Retail Associate*
Furniture Salesman	*Disneyland Coin Operated Video Game Mechanic*

No, I never got commissions. No employee discount. Not even a special thanks from management.

But what *did* I get?

An encounter that otherwise would not have existed. And that's a big part of understanding approachability. The only reason I engaged with customers was because they asked me for help. They wanted to learn about products or, in one instance, karate lessons. Not just because I was wearing a nametag, but because I was **ready to engage**. They chose to approach me to acquire that information – **Engagement Motivator #2** – to *learn*. This is what I call being Open for Business. (More on this in Chapter 8)

Let me ask you this...

When you have a question, how do you decide who to approach to help?

PERSONALITY TYPE #5: THE HERO – 5%

One evening my friend Laszlo and I went out to dinner at a upscale restaurant in Portland. The ambiance was just as stunning as our Zagat Restaurant Guide depicted. (We may have been a little underdressed.)

"How many zis evening?" the host asked.

"There will be two of us. Do you have an open table?" asked Laszlo.

The host sidled up to me, got 6 *inches* from my face, pointed at my nametag and POKED my chest! He then rudely said, "Excuse me Scott – do you really want to wear zee nametag during zee dinner?"

You MUST be joking.

At this point he had committed three Interpersonal Violations:

1. Intimate Space (18 inches) – GONE!
2. Safety from Touch (my chest) – GONE!
3. Personal Property (my nametag) – GONE!

I couldn't believe the nerve of this jerk. I glared at him as seriously as possible and said, "Yes, sir. I have a serious short term memory condition. Is that a problem for you?"

"Eh...no...but of course sir! Eh...please wait at zee bar while I get zee table."

We waited at the bar – for about twenty seconds! Then we decided any establishment so pretentious and unwilling to accept customers for their differences did not deserve our business.

So we went to McDonald's.

This personality type poses yet another interesting question about approachability: **is there a price to pay for "throwing yourself out there"?**

Absolutely. When you make yourself more open and ready to engage with those around you, be prepared to deal with a few Naysayers. The Haters. The people who don't accept your willingness to stand out and break the silence.

In my case; I encounter people who don't like and/or accept my willingness to open the lines of communication. That's the reason they are called *The Heros*. **They attempt to rescue me** from doing something stupid, i.e., wearing a nametag all the time.

Here's another *Hero* example from 36,000 feet above the air. My flight was returning to St. Louis from a National Speakers Association convention in Phoenix. I was trying hard to concentrate on some writing, when, out of nowhere, the flight attendant walked up to me, slapped my chest/nametag, laughed and walked away! And because I was deeply immersed in my creative thoughts – I jumped so high I nearly hit my head on the television screen!

But I didn't make a fuss. After four plus years I've become accustomed to these violations. Yet, I've never come to understand this phenomenon: why is it that complete strangers feel it's acceptable to touch, slap, poke and pull on my nametag, when it would be just as easy to simply say, "Scott, do you know you're still wearing your nametag?"

Luckily for the flight attendant, she happened to violate someone extremely friendly and forgiving who didn't call the airline with a customer complaint.

On the other hand:

> *"Make a customer happy and he'll tell five people. Make a customer upset and he'll tell twenty people. But make a speaker and a writer upset, and he'll tell thousands of people for the next 20 years every time he gives a speech or writes a book."*
>
> — SCOTT GINSBERG

Although this personality type is the least common of all, the link between this group of people and the motivators of human engagement is astounding. The flight attendant's goal in slapping my chest – which, legally could have been reported as sexual harassment – was to "minister to my needs," i.e., **Engagement Motivator #1** – *to help*. To her, my needs were to be "rescued and reminded" I was wearing a nametag and to have my nametag removed before I suffered further loss of face. Unbelievable!

Anyway, that incident is in the past. I don't want to call needless attention to the actual name of the flight attendant or the particular airline in the text of this book. (See reference below)[1]

But in addition to "rescuing" me, these two encounters with *The Hero* (the restaurant and the airplane) taught me about approachability in a few ways. Both the host and the flight attendant wanted to remove my nametag for the purposes of conforming me to an appearance code acceptable in the eyes of their establishment. (Unfortunately, they did so a rude, violating manners.) In other words, they engaged for the purposes of control, manipulation and direction, i.e., **Engagement Motivator #4** – *to influence.*

Let me ask you this...
Has anyone ever tried to stop you from standing out or being different?

All day, every day for over four years – that's a lot of nametags! What's more, that's a lot of encounters. As you saw from the questions I posed at the end of each personality type, *The Inquirer, The Player, The Joker, The Customer* and *The Hero* symbolized that approachability truly is a **two way street:** you must approach others, and you must be approachable to others.

POWER PRINCIPLE #1
BEING APPROACHABLE MEANS BEING READY TO ENGAGE

If you consider the reactions and stories in this chapter, most people would NEVER want to wear a nametag all the time. Especially with some

[1] Gloria Paulson, American Airlines Flight 2886 from PHX to STL, July 21, 2004, 9:51 PM EDT

of the more violating *Hero* incidents, I will say I don't encourage everyone to wear nametags.

In fact, on my website (www.hellomynameisscott.com) the disclaimer reads:

> *Front Porch Productions does not recommend or encourage all people to wear nametags. Although nametags can be successful tools for encouraging others to be friendlier; nametags may be potentially dangerous for anyone whose anonymity is vital to their own personal safety.*

So, wearing a nametag is merely *one way* to encourage people to become more approachable. It's *one* way to throw yourself out there. Not the *only* way.

I think of my nametag as my **front porch**. And because the goal of this book is to help you become the epitome of approachability, let's move on to Chapter 2. We'll define what a **front porch** is, and how you can use it to become a more effective, engaging communicator – one conversation at a time.

If the World Had a Front Porch

The Epitome of Approachability

"The front porch was an invention of the housewife
who wanted to keep her husband far enough away from house;
but close enough so she could yell if she needed him to lift something heavy."
BILL COSBY

IN APRIL OF 2003 DURING A SHORT VISIT TO THE BIG APPLE, I TOOK A WALK around New York City's Battery Park. I noticed a man sitting on a bench feeding nuts to some squirrels. I looked at him, he looked at my nametag and then he waved me over.

"Hey Scott, come sit down next to me! Feed the squirrels – it's so much fun!"

I was hesitant at first, but he was smiling and seemed like a nice old guy, so I walked toward him.

"It's OK Scott; I'll show you how to do it!"

As I sat down he placed a nut in my right hand. He then told me to hold my left palm up and wait. And before I could say "rabid street rodent," I felt a thud on my back.

A squirrel then scurried across my chest and crept onto my hand!

Oh my God. There's a squirrel on my hand! Don't these little buggers carry rabies!?

"Don't squirrels carry rabies?" I asked the man.

"No, they're quite tame and friendly. I've been doing this for 20 years and I promise they'll be nice to you! In fact, this particular squirrel here, his name is Joey!"

He went on to tell me tales of squirrels from years ago, his life story and great friends he made over the years. He knew everything about the

types of squirrels, their eating habits and names of about fifty regulars who always showed up!

"I buy about 4 pounds of nuts a day," he said, "and I'm out here 4-6 days a week. I just love to invite new people to say hello. I make friends from around the world! Anyway, my name's Ira, but everyone knows me as The Squirrel Man."

That's an example of a **front porch.** And a front porch is the most important tool you can use to become a more effective, engaging communicator – one conversation at a time.

Let's begin this chapter with my definition. A **front porch** is:

Any object or behavior that increases approachability.

Notice the dichotomy – *object* or *behavior.* As you will learn from various examples throughout the book, both are equally effective. For example, my front porch (a nametag) happens to be an object. A thing. A little piece of paper. But you'll find that a front porch can be something as simple as a few kind words or even a friendly gesture.[1]

✦ ✦ ✦ ✦ ✦

Front porches were first made popular by the Greeks. They used them as gathering spots for public discussions, originally called *porticos.* Then, thousands of years later in the South, the front porch evolved into a symbol of community, hospitality and friendliness.

A few years ago when I began giving speeches about approachability, I discovered a connection between nametags and front porches. I thought back to *The Inquirer, The Player, The Joker, The Customer* and *The Hero.* Each person manifested approachability by **engaging** with me.

But what were they *really* doing?

First of all they became friendlier, more sociable and willing to communicate. I experienced encounters that never would have occurred otherwise. Also, my nametag offered a free ticket for conversation and extended hospitality. This ultimately made people feel more comfortable interacting with me. So essentially, my nametag – as a tool to encourage people to communicate – *was my front porch!* After all, a front porch is nothing but an architectural manifestation of the interpersonal concept of approachability.

[1] Or a wild rodent

CHARACTERISTICS OF FRONT PORCHES

Before you begin building front porches, you must first understand how they *expedite* the communication process.

A front porch *creates comfort.* Discomfort and uncertainty stem from a lack of information. This is the number one reason conversations are avoided. In other words, the less you know, the less you say. Conversely, the more you know about someone or the situation, the more comfortable you become. Let's go back to my encounter with Ira the Squirrel Guy. Considering he was a strange old man sitting on a park bench in the middle of New York City, I'd say he did an excellent job of making a complete stranger feel comfortable!

A front porch *breaks the ice.* In 2003 I received an email from a woman named Lauren, one of my newsletter subscribers and a former student from Auburn University. According to her, every October 23rd, it's "Hey Day" on campus. As a play on words, it's a day when students and faculty give special notice to Auburn's reputation for being a friendly campus. And on this day, everyone always smiles and says "Hey!" to each other – even when they don't know the person! ("Hey Day" has since been adopted by several other colleges around the nation.)

That's a front porch.

As I noted in Chapter 1, breaking the ice is often the most difficult part of any conversation. According to the SP/SAA (Social Phobia/Social Anxiety Association)[2] people are terrified of striking up conversations with strangers because of the **fear of rejection**. But with a front porch, this fear is minimized.

A front porch also *builds rapport.* While more detailed examples of front porches will be used throughout the book, I still think a **smile** is the simplest *behavioral* front porch because it's the number one interpersonal signal that conversation is desirable. I once read in a 2004 survey conducted by Impulse Research Corporation, which polled more than 1,500 people nationwide, half of the participants reported that a smile was the most common indicator of approachability!

Here's one of my favorite examples. One November my friend Liz went to the grocery store to pick up a turkey for Thanksgiving. As she approached the checkout, she noticed the cashier's nametag, smiled and said, "Hi Jenny – Happy Thanksgiving!"

Jenny smiled back at Liz and swiped her turkey. When she gave her the total, Liz couldn't help but notice an unusually low price.

[2] www.socialphobia.org

"I thought the price was more than that...is this turkey on sale or something?" Liz asked.

"No, it's not on sale," Jenny replied, "But I always give 30% discounts to customers who smile at me!"

That's a front porch.

(I now shop there every week)

A front porch *empowers people to communicate.* Although we all possess the inherent desire to interact with each other, sometimes we still need the smallest push to get the ball rolling. Once during a speech at a local meeting in St. Louis, I noticed an audience member was wearing a bright yellow pin which read: CONQUER THE MOMENT.

I approached the man, glanced at his nametag and said, "Brian, tell us what CONQUER THE MOMENT is all about..."

"Well," Brian explained, "I always wear this pin to remind people that every single moment we have on this earth is a gift from God. We must take advantage of every opportunity to maximize our potential by conquering the moment. Because if the moment passes and we fail to take initiative; *it conquers us.*"

That's a front porch.

This is a classic example of wearing pins to empower communication. Think of the various pins and accessories you've seen or worn over the years: political, musical, spiritual, sports related or humorous – all are great front porches! (See Appendix B: 52 Ways to Build Front Porches)

Let me ask you this...

What could you say to someone wearing an eye catching accessory?

The final key to front porches is they can be **built by anyone, anywhere.** Even in the most unlikely situations. I learned this last lesson in approachability several years ago while driving down the highway.

Have you ever seen these stickers on Jeeps that read "It's a Jeep thing...you wouldn't understand"? Unless you actually have a Jeep, you probably respond the same way I do: *I don't get it.*

Exactly. Non-Jeep owners have no idea what these stickers mean. But recently I got the inside track on this unwritten Jeep rule.

For years, online stores, shops, catalogues and dealers encouraged Jeep owners to show their pride and enthusiasm with these officially licensed "It's a Jeep thing ... you wouldn't understand" accessories. Contrary to popular belief, however, they have little to do with marketing, brand arrogance or the intent to confuse the heck out of other drivers stuck in rush hour traffic. In truth, it's all about creating community!

Once, my cousin Justin and I were enjoying a beautiful summer day while cruising around in his Wrangler. He told me that since he started driving his Jeep over the summer, he was greeted and waved to by more motorists on the road than ever before! *And they were always other Jeep owners.* Each time they waved to one another as if to say, "Hey, nice Jeep ... brother."

It's just like the old saying goes, "Birds of a feather drive together."

These examples are just a few of my favorite front porches. Whether it's a squirrel, a smile, a pin, a "Hey!" or a Jeep, all of these objects and behaviors contain one similarity:

POWER PRINCIPLE #1
BEING APPROACHABLE
MEANS BEING ACCESSIBLE
AND EASY TO DEAL WTIH

As we finish this chapter, let me share with you one last story about the first time I attended my local Chamber of Commerce Meeting as a small business owner. A lady at my table introduced herself to me and asked what company I was with. Now, because I had just started my business that month – this was the first time anyone ever asked me that question. I told her, "Front Porch Productions."

"Hmm...Front Porch Productions – well Scott, what exactly do you do, *build front porches?*"

"Yes! In fact, that's *exactly* what I do – I build front porches!" And that's exactly what we're going to do to in the rest of this book – we're going to build front porches. But, before we move on, let's review what we've already learned about this new concept:

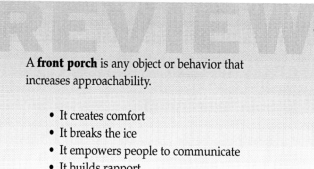

A **front porch** is any object or behavior that increases approachability.

- It creates comfort
- It breaks the ice
- It empowers people to communicate
- It builds rapport
- It can be built by anyone, anywhere

Let's move on to Chapter 3 where you will learn how to use front porches to make UNFORGETTABLE™ first impressions.

CHAPTER THREE

UNFORGETTABLE™ First Impressions, Part 1

How to Be Open for Business

"I'm like a mirror –
I'm nothing till you look at me."

MARK SANDMAN OF MORPHINE

YOU NEVER GET A SECOND CHANCE TO MAKE A FIRST IMPRESSION.

You've heard this phrase a million times, right?

Me too – and I don't like it. It puts too much pressure on us. And every time someone says it you think, "Duh! Of course I only have one chance! Thanks for reminding me! Now I'm self-conscious and I'm probably going to blow it!"

Don't worry. In the next two chapters, you will learn a system called "UNFORGETTABLE™," which examines six essential elements for flawless first impressions.[1] In this chapter, we'll focus on **Part 1**: *How to Be Open for Business*, in which you will learn the first three elements:

1) Time is Not On Your Side

2) Build Front Porches

3) Break Down Barriers

GOOD NEWS: *You never get a second chance to make a first impression* is a sentence that will soon be eliminated from your vocabulary. Because after you work through this system, **you won't NEED a second chance to make a first impression**. More importantly, you won't make a *good* first impression; you'll make an UNFORGETTABLE™ first impression!

ESSENTIAL ELEMENT FOR FLAWLESS FIRST IMPRESSIONS #1
TIME IS NOT ON YOUR SIDE

You only have three seconds...Connect in under a minute...People decide if they like you within the first ninety seconds... It's all about the first five seconds...You get the job within four minutes...Always make a friend in less than 30 seconds...

Ahhhhhhhhhh!! Which one is right!?

I've read almost every book on first impressions, and the primary issue addressed tends to be **time.** (Or lack thereof.) Unfortunately, past research doesn't offer much consistency among increments of time in which you must make a first impression.

So, I'm not going to give you a specific number of minutes, hours, days or milliseconds to which your words and actions must adhere in order to "wow" the other person. The bottom line is this: **every situation and every person is different**. Only you can decide how much time

---

[1] This system is based on Scott's 60 minute audio program called "UNFORGETTABLE," available on www.hellomynameisscott.com

you're allotted before your conversation partner thinks you're the greatest person they've ever met.

Still, you have to work quickly if you want to be UNFORGETTABLE™!

First impressions span beyond initial contact. Because they are based on instinct and emotion; and because they are usually correct; first impressions people form about you will probably stay in their minds forever because people put pressure on themselves to behave consistently with their own existing commitments. And as the great poet William Hazlit said, "First impressions are a person's work of years; they are stamped on his face by the events of his whole life by the hand of nature, and are not to be gotten rid of easily."

First impressions also form because of the *primacy effect*. In other words, the first information people see or learn about you is more powerful than what is learned later. Therefore, when people initially see a small piece of you, that's all they know. So to them, it represents everything.

And first impressions aren't just the *first time* you meet someone; they're also the first time you *have* with someone. So, even if you've already known someone – your first impression, new or not, will still set the stage for whatever communication comes next.

Here's an example. Let's say you arrive (late) at your customer's office for your monthly appointment and you're in a terrible mood. You're tired, annoyed and don't feel like crunching numbers. Now, even if you've worked with this customer for six months, it's still possible to make a bad first impression. It's still possible turn him off. And as a result, your entire meeting might be underscored by that negative impression regardless of what the customer thought of you six months ago when he first met you.

In short, first doesn't always mean *first time*.

A final point about the time of constraints of first impressions is honesty: **it's always the best policy**. It's like the old joke says, "If you tell the truth, you won't need to remember anything." In your first impressions, be honest and be honest immediately.

Once during a job interview I had the perfect opportunity to practice this last rule. My potential boss said, "All right Scott, here's the last question, and it's kind of a tough one. In fact, most employees struggle to answer it...so just do your best:

"What are some of your weaknesses?"

Ouch. A zinger if I ever heard one. Looked like my ego was about to take a beating.

But I didn't skip a beat. I smiled, re-crossed my legs and said, "Absolutely! In fact, I'll give you three of them:

1) I talk too much. As an extrovert, my personality is such that I might never shut up.

2) I'm not the most punctual employee in the world. I've been known to show up at the last minute, or sometimes a few minutes late.

3) I'm a big goofball. I do, say and think things that are outlandish.

But I'll tell you one thing," I added, "talking, tardiness and goofiness – all of those habits can change. But the one quality about me that will never change…is my **honesty**, and THAT is exactly why you need to hire me."

The room fell silent. And do you know what two words came out of his mouth next?

Get out.

No, I'm just kidding! He said, "Welcome aboard!"

UNFORGETTABLE™, indeed.

ESSENTIAL ELEMENT FOR FLAWLESS FIRST IMPRESSIONS #2
USE FRONT PORCHES

I walked into Pottery Barn about a year ago for nothing in particular, just to browse. The first person who greeted me was an employee wearing a string of large red plastic chili peppers around her neck. I immediately saw a great opportunity to talk to her, so I commented about it.

"I like your necklace!" I joked.

(Obviously the decoration was traditionally used for a kitchen, but this employee wanted to have some fun with the accessory.)

"It's not really a necklace," she explained, "but I guess this accessory is whatever you want it to be."

I commented about her creative conversation starter. We went on to talk about a variety of communication related topics for the next twenty minutes. And although I didn't buy anything that day, on every occasion I visited the store, I always came back and talked to Sioux. She made such an UNFORGETTABLE™ first impression on me that, if I ever needed anything I had a friend who was willing to help. I became a loyal customer.

As you learned in Chapter 2, your *front porch* is any object or behavior that increases approachability. What's more, your **front porch is the easiest way to become UNFORGETTABLE™!**

POWER PRINCIPLE #3

BEING APPROACHABLE MEANS BEING AVAILABLE TO OTHERS

Now, obviously we can't all wear nametags or chili peppers wherever we go. So let's examine some other front porch *behaviors* to help you maintain approachability for a flawless first impression.

In your conversations and interactions, being approachable means you set the tone for the interaction. To do this, you must combine two factors: **mood** and **engagement**. With the Pottery Barn example, you saw how powerful engagement was to connect two people. But another effective way to build front porches is with your answers to ritual, mundane questions, or "Fruitless Questions," as I like to call them. This has an amazing effect on the mood.

I used to work with a guy named Henry. He was the overnight bellman at the Ritz Carlton in St. Louis (before he retired). You couldn't miss this guy: fifty five years old, six-foot-six and always with a smile on his face!

One evening at 11 PM sharp, I walked through the front door and noticed Henry strutting in my direction. As he passed by, I quickly glanced at his nametag and said hello, "Hi Henry, how ya' doin?"

I'll never forget what he said next: *"Everything is beautiful!"*

Wow. Awfully chipper for someone about to work 11 PM – 7 AM, wouldn't you say? I later discovered Henry had been the overnight bellman for more than 10 years. He strutted into work every night at 11:00 PM, and didn't leave until every shoe was polished, every bag was delivered and every guest got his USA Today. And Henry always had a smile on his face.

Here's the cool part: when I returned home later that night, I opened the fridge to get a drink of water. At least, I *thought* it was water. But because I am, in fact, a man, I started to drink right out of the pitcher...

Glug...glug...glug...

Ahhh! Lemonade! My cheeks tingled from the surprising tart flavor as I gulped down an unexpected swig of Country Time. Woooo-weee! That woke me up at one in the morning!

I then realized Henry's answer was just like that pitcher of lemonade.

Think about your responses to fruitless, ritual, mundane questions like "How are you?" "What's up?" "How's business?" or "How *you* doin?" (If you live in New York City.)

What's your answer? Good? Great? Ok? Not bad?

Guess what? Those answers are BOR-ing! They offer limited spice to your encounters. And most of the time, people use them as fast getaways to be polite, say hello, and get on with their isolated lives.

But, when it comes to conversation, Henry's response is the perfect example of how to give "Flavored Answers to Fruitless Questions." Here's what I mean...

When you offer a **flavored** answer (*Everything is beautiful*) to a **fruitless** question (*How are you?*), it magnetizes people. It makes you more approachable. People won't be able to resist talking to you because you will be so *darn sweet*! In other words, you will turn water into lemonade.

Great example: A few months ago I was eating at a restaurant in St. Louis called Ozzie's, named after the great Cardinals shortstop. This is where I first met Cherise.

"Good afternoon, my name is Cherise – how are you today?"

"Not bad, how about yourself?"

"I'm blessed, thanks for asking!"

Wait a sec. Did she just say "blessed"?

"Excuse me Cherise, but did you say 'blessed'?"

"Yes I did! I'm just so fortunate to be blessed in all areas of my life and I love to share that with all of my customers!"

Wow! *That's* a flavored answer. I inquired further about Cherise's "blessed" life and discovered she was not only a waitress but a musician who was in the process of signing her first record contract.

Yet again, another UNFORGETTBALE™ first impression.

My final example – a flavored answer of business – comes from my friend Jeffery Gitomer. I once helped out at one of his sales seminars when his speaking tour came into my city. During one of the modules in his presentation, Jeffery spoke about the use of positive sales verbiage. He asked the audience to chorally respond to mundane questions like "How is business?" or "What's new with work?"

Most members in the audience yelled "Business is slow," "It's picking up," or "Well, the economy is down."

"Your answers are no good!!" Jeffery said.

"You're in sales to make money!" he continued, "So when someone asks 'How is business?' say something like, "Cashin' checks baby!"

Now, keep in mind Jeffery isn't your typical salesman, so his answers won't work for everybody. But his flavored responses are *honest, open and funny*. And because Jeffery is one of my friends, I will attest that as a person, he is honest, open and funny. Therefore his answers also **personify his attitude**.

As you can see, "Everything is beautiful!" "Blessed" and "Cashin' checks baby!" immediately made Henry, Cherise and Jeffery more approachable. And with something as simple as using friendly and positive words, I always felt comfortable stepping onto THEIR front porch.

So, next time someone utters, "How are you?" or "What's up?" think about your flavored answer. (You'll learn more specifically how to do this in Chapter 5) Come up with something creative and surprising that personifies your attitude, and makes you easy and to deal with. I guarantee it will magnetize people. This behavior will not only make you more approachable, but your first impression will be UNFORGETTABLE™.

Let me ask you this...
What's your flavored answer to
"How are you?"

ESSENTIAL ELEMENT FOR FLAWLESS FIRST IMPRESSIONS #3
BREAK DOWN BARRIERS

In the process of becoming UNFORGETTABLE™ in your first impressions, beware of communication barriers – they can ruin your chances! In this third section, we will examine the **Top Ten Most Dangerous Communication Barriers** that stand in your way of making flawless first impressions.

COMMUNICATION BARRIER #1: Monosyllabic Conversation Killers

As we've just discussed, most people answer mundane, ritual (fruitless) questions like "How are ya?" "What's up?" or "How you doin?" with such monosyllabic conversation killers like "Fine," "Good," "Ok" and "Ehh…" But these answers imply you don't care enough to tell people how you really feel.

I recently had a close call with this one.

Did you ever watch that scene in *Indiana Jones and the Temple of Doom* where Harisson Ford was trapped on a chicken infested cargo plane with no pilot, speeding towards a mountain that awaited his fiery death?

Great! Now you know how I felt during flight 7026 from Colorado Springs to Denver in the summer of 2004.

I was returning back to St. Louis after giving a speech to a youth leadership camp. And I can honestly say; it was the scariest flight of my life. Now, I didn't think I was going to die. I was actually quite relaxed through some breathing and meditating exercises I've learned over the years. But after I rushed out of the plane, stepped onto the runway and thanked the Almighty God for sparing my life, I realized something: I felt like hell. My head was pounding. I needed Advil, and I needed it like, twenty minutes ago.

I rushed to the first newsstand I saw and grabbed a few single servings of ibuprofen. I placed them on the counter and pulled out my wallet.

"How are you today sir?" the clerk asked.

"Good."

Good?

"No…wait. I'm sorry. You know what? I'm really not good – in fact, I feel terrible. *I just took the worst flight of my life!* But I'm SO glad I raced to this store as soon as possible for some Advil. Sorry I gave you a canned answer."

"Well, at least you're honest!" he said.

"Yeah, well…I just couldn't sit here and tell you I was 'good' when in fact, I was not. You deserve for me to be truthful."

Often times, we get so rushed and programmed in our routines – especially our verbal responses to ritual questions – we become blind to traces of inauthenticity.

Next time someone asks, "How are you?" tell him how you really feel. Be honest AND positive. You will be amazed how great of a first impression you will make.

COMMUNICATION BARRIER #2: Hands Are Full

Whether you're at a networking event, a bar, a party or a meeting, always carry your stuff in your left hand. This keeps your right hand accessible for handshakes, introductions and the like. When someone approaches you – whether you know her or not – you don't want to fumble with your belongings. Make the handshake smooth and quick.

What's more, with your right hand available – you offer an act of kindness to the other person. There's nothing worse than the feeling of getting left hanging from a handshake or high five that didn't happen.

COMMUNICATION BARRIER #3: One-Uppers

Every so often, you'll have a conversation with someone who insists on interrupting AND competing with everything you do and say. For example:

* "You just went on a cruise? Really! I've already been on three this year! My wife and I went down to Nassau and saw the most beautiful..."
* "Wow, a 12% increase in sales huh? Yeah, *my* company increased about 19% after the sales team landed the biggest account since..."
* "Oh, that's your girlfriend over there? She's cute. Which reminds me, did you meet my girlfriend Inga...the runway model? Let me introduce you..."

You know how this kind of interruption/condescension makes you feel. And you don't want others with whom you interact to feel the same. But at the same time you do want to participate in the conversation and overcome this barrier. A suggestion is to give a "me too" statement, followed by a follow up question. This allows you to participate AND get the other person back on track. Now, this doesn't actually mean you say "me too." But it's easy to let the other person know how you relate to the topic without stealing their thunder.

For example:

* "Yes, I've always enjoyed cruises too. Where did you go?"
* "Wow! Looks like business is good for both of us! What's coming up next for your company?"
* "Glad to see your girlfriend came with you tonight – I love when mine joins me. How long have you two been together?"

Using a "me too" statement manifests synchronicity. It's a form of reactive positioning that, when phrased correctly, doesn't show superiority. And it *doesn't* interrupt them.

> *"Taking the conversation away from another person is a common form of*
>
> *lack of self control which is not only discourteous, but it deprives those*
>
> *who do it of many valuable opportunities to learn from others."*
>
> NAPOLEON HILL

COMMUNICATION BARRIER #4: The BBD (Bigger, Better Deal)

I first experienced the BBD when I joined my local Chamber of Commerce. I was talking to a lady who gave me some tips on how to get the most out of the organization when, not one minute into our conversation, I realized she wasn't even looking at me anymore! We kept talking but she constantly scanned the room not unlike a bobble head doll in search of someone else who was a) more interesting, b) more exciting and c) more likely to buy her products than me.

Ouch.

I understand the importance of meeting new prospects at networking events – especially where there's limited time. But it is possible to excuse yourself from a conversation without making your partner feel puny and insignificant.

Simply say: *"I've enjoyed talking with you, but I need to speak with some other people. I hope we can catch up later!"*

COMMUNICATION BARRIER #5: Monopolize the Conversation

I once gave a speech to a large audience at a book fair in St. Louis. After the program was over there was a book signing, during which I had the pleasure of meeting many wonderful audience members. One in particular was a friend of my Grandmother's. She couldn't have been sweeter. Unfortunately, because of time constraints, several people in line became frustrated when Eva insisted on talking to me for well over 10 minutes!

She had the *monopoly* on the conversation.

People don't always do this consciously, however it's extremely difficult to communicate when such a barrier is raised. If it happens to you, the most appropriate way to handle it is similar to the "Bigger, Better Deal." You must gracefully bow out of the conversation. Also tell them if they'd like to talk again later, you'll be around – but you want to be fair and make yourself open to everyone. Remember, first impressions revolve around *approachability*, so it's not fair to you OR to other people if your time is monopolized.

COMMUNICATION BARRIER #6: The Green Teeth Theory

Has someone ever told you there was something in your teeth – four hours after you ate? It made you wonder how gross your smile looked all night. It also made you wonder, "Would I tell someone if he had something in his teeth?"

Yes. Always tell people when there's something stuck in their teeth. Now, you don't want to embarrass someone in front of a group by saying something like, "Hey Paul, are you saving that piece for dessert?" There is a proper way to do this. Take the person aside and politely tell him:

a) He has a small (or enormous) piece of food in his teeth

b) Where it's exactly located, i.e., between the front two teeth

c) If he successful removed it

The Green Teeth Theory also applies to clothes, spelling errors or any other faux pas someone needs to know about. When you inform people of this information, it allows them save face and enhances *their* ability to make UNFORGETTABLE™ first impressions thereafter. And I guarantee they will thank you for this tip every time. Besides, better they get embarrassed in front of you than eight other people at the table.

Let me ask you this...

If you had green stuff in your teeth, wouldn't you want to know?

COMMUNICATION BARRIER #7: Opening with Insults

As I noted in Chapter 1, I get made fun of between 3-5 times a day for wearing a nametag everywhere I go. (It's a small price to pay for throwing yourself out there!) But it's amazing how often people will insult me as a conversation starter. *Especially in front of other people.* As if this was an effective way to make a good first impression.

- "Hey Scott, take off that stupid nametag!"
- "So Scott, do you have a memory problem or something?"

Similarly, I've heard people insult others behind their back just to start a conversation.

- "Ughh...look at that woman's dress! Who is she kidding? Maybe she should try the next size up. Anyway, my name is Kate, what's your name?"

It is impossible to make a good first impression if you begin your conversation with an insult.

COMMUNICATION BARRIER #8: Forgetting Names

I was watching a basketball game at my neighborhood Cheers-esque bar when I noticed my old friend Tina sitting across the room. I approached her and said hello. She then introduced me to her friend sitting next to her.

"Scott, this is my friend Lauren."

"Hello Lauren, nice to meet you..."

Lauren and I talked for a few minutes as she told me about her job. She then asked about my job, so I told her about some articles I was working on. Asked if I had written anything recently, I told Lauren about an article that ran in the February 2004 issue of the St. Louis Small Business Monthly called "10 Effective Ways to Remember Someone's Name." (See Appendix E)

"I'm soooo bad at names," Lauren said, "I wish I had some good ways to remember them."

Recognizing an opportunity to help someone out – and possibly impress a cute girl – I recited the summary of my article and gave Lauren a few pointers on ways to recall names. I felt that as an expert, I could help her.

After I finished my five minute rant, I patted Lauren on the shoulder, smiled and confidently said, "You know, *Stacey...*"

"Whoa...wait a minute....WHAT did you just call me?!" She exclaimed.

Oh no.

"Ummm...Sta...cey?" I muttered under my breath.

"Yeah...my name's Lauren, NOT Stacey.

Nice one Scott.

"You know, *Scott,* maybe you should re-read your own article sometime!"

Touche, Lauren. Or was it Stacey?

This was the most embarrassing, hypocritical moment of my life. Also, do you remember when we talked about the **lasting effect** of first impressions in the beginning of this chapter? Well, every once in a while I run into Stacey/Lauren – and she usually greets me with a sarcastic scowl.

So much for making a flawless first impression!

As I've already discussed, a person's name is the sweetest sound he or she will ever hear. But here's a fact few people know, and it comes from no less an authority than Sigmund Freud:

A person's name is the single context of human memory most apt to be forgotten.

Ironic, huh?

I suggest the adjective association technique to recall names. In all of the books on name memory I've read, this seems to be the most effective. When you meet someone new, take their name and match it with a personal characteristic that starts with the same letter.

- Bright Bridget
- Loud Lori
- Seven Foot Seth

The key to this technique is to use an association as ridiculous as possible. It doesn't even have to make sense, as long as you remember it. **That which is outrageous and exaggerated is memorable.** (For more tips, please refer to Appendix D: "Why Can't I Remember Your Name?")

COMMUNICATION BARRIER #9: Business Cards

Here's a phrase you must eliminate from your vocabulary:

"I don't have any of my business cards with me right now."

I am amazed how often this happens. With this one sentence, people immediately put up barriers to communication. Especially at networking meetings or other events, not having business cards gives the impression that people don't care enough about the meeting or event to come prepared.

> *"But I ran out of cards and the new batch is at the print shop*
> *and I'm going to pick them up today and I*
> *swear I'll write your name down and..."*

No good. You need them now. More importantly, someone else needs them now. (This problem will be solved later in Chapter 7 when you learn how to become a Networking Superhero.)

Think about your printer: when it gets low on toner, what happens? That little window pops up to remind you to order a new cartridge, right? This is a valuable feature, especially if you've ever been in the middle of printing out a 200 page manuscript for your first book at 5:00 AM when Copy Nation on Main Street was closed for repairs and your deadline was approaching 3 hours later. (Hypothetically, of course.)

But just like printing, making a first impression is an on-demand project. You never know when you'll need to be UNFORGETTABLE™.

If you don't have your business cards with you at all times, you won't make a *bad* impression — you'll make NO impression.

COMMUNICATION BARRIER #10: Follow Through

Finally, if you say you're going call, CALL. If you say you're going to email, EMAIL. It doesn't matter if it's business, with friends, a date or an appointment with the dentist. If you want to make an UNFORGETTABLE™ first impression, be known as someone "who always follows through."

At a speaker's conference in 2003 I had the pleasure of watching an amazing sales/customer service trainer. After her presentation I tried my hardest to make my way to the front of the room, but due to the crowd – I didn't have a chance to talk to her.

"Oh well," I thought, "I'll just drop her a line next week."

I emailed her the following Monday with a message filled with praise. I explained how much I learned from her program. I even quoted her speech regarding to her system for **treating customers appreciatively**, and then asked her to write back so we could chat for a few minutes.

I never heard from her. Ever. Perhaps my message got "lost in the mail somewhere." Interestingly enough, I later found out that several friends of mine had similar problems trying to contact her.

And out the window went my impression of *her*.

✦ ✦ ✦ ✦ ✦

Before we move on to the second part of the UNFORGETTABLE™ system, let's review the first three Essential Elements of Flawless First Impressions:

Time is Not on Your Side – beware of limited time you have to make a first impression

Use Front Porches – use objects and behaviors to increase approachability so people feel comfortable and empowered to communicate

Break Down Barriers – beware of closing yourself off with negative attitudes and actions

CHAPTER FOUR

UNFORGETTABLE™ First Impressions, Part 2

Go From HOW Are You to WHO Are You

"People may not remember exactly what you did,
or what you said, but they will always
remember how you made them feel."

MOTHER THERESA

UNFORGETTABLE™ FIRST IMPRESSIONS ARE NOT JUST ABOUT BEING OPEN FOR business – they're also about showing interest. In other words, **going from HOW are you to WHO are you.**

ESSENTIAL ELEMENT FOR FLAWLESS FIRST IMPRESSIONS #4
DISCOVER THE CPI (COMMON POINT OF INTEREST)

People like others whom they are like. If you want to make a flawless first impression, it is your duty to discover what you have in common with every person you talk to by discovering the **CPI, or Common Point of Interest.**

I'll never forget the moment I discovered how valuable Common Points of Interest were to first impressions. One evening, my friend Mitch and I were introduced to a small group of people at a local restaurant. To my dismay, the conversation didn't get off to an exciting start. In fact, it was downright boring! But I wanted to be sure the encounter with our new friends was engaging, so I offered one of my favorite questions to ask new people:

"What's your favorite cereal?"

Mitch and I got a mild chuckle from the group, but eventually everyone contributed. We then talked for twenty minutes about more in depth, personal topics like childhood memories and growing up eating our favorite cereals. What a great conversation!

At the end of the night, Mitch and I said goodbye to our new friends. And on the way out, they actually thanked us for one of the best conversations they'd had in months!

Fast forward...

A few weeks later I ran into Anne, one of the girls from the table I met that night. She jumped out of her seat and gave me a hearty greeting!

"Hey nice to see you again Scott! My friends and I still talk about how enjoyable our cereal conversation was with you and Mitch. We'll never forget that!"

This is the first way to discover the CPI, or Common Point of Interest: **asking open ended questions** (Excellent front porches). These are questions that don't elicit *yes, no* or the popular emotional smokescreen, "Fine." In fact, did you know that "Fine" is NOT found in the dictionary? It's true! I've spent several years looking this word up in different dictionaries, and it turns out that "Fine" is actually an acronym for:

<u>F</u>EELINGS

<u>I</u>'M

<u>N</u>OT

<u>E</u>XPRESSING

Think about it: are you fine? Have you ever been fine? **In the history of conversation**, has anyone ever been "Fine"? No. But it's an easy answer. Especially to an easy question. So, instead of saying how they really feel, people take the easy way out. They take the "Fine" way out.

But it might not be their fault, though. Maybe the **wrong questions** were asked.

When you meet someone for the first time, pose questions that begin with "What's your favorite...?" "How long have you been...?" and "How did you get started...?" Questions like these build rapport, spark creativity and invite others to share experiences and preferences. What's more, they show interest in people's opinions and insights. (See Appendix A: 55 Great Questions to Ask Someone You Just Met)

What people LIKE is just as important as what they ARE LIKE.

Another way to discover the CPI is with **compliments**. If you want to be UNFORGETTABLE™ in your first impressions, giving a compliment – and doing so effectively – is a fail safe method. And I'm not talking about cheap flattery. There is a right and wrong way to do this. If someone came up to you and said, "Hey, uh...you're cute!" or "You smell good," would you feel flattered? Would you feel like he or she took an interest in you? Probably not. Stuff like that just shows someone is looking for an easy way in.

But there's a simple and effective way to structure a compliment – without sounding like you're kissing butt. Compliments have to be specific or else they don't sound heartfelt. Also, adding an open ended question after your compliment will encourage others to offer more information about themselves. For example: "That's an elegant watch. Where is it from?"

Specifically when you compliment accessories, clothing and the like, ask people **where they got something**. It's a great way to get a story or some background information. How many times have you asked someone this question who answered with something like "...when I was on vacation"? Answers like these always generate a synchronized, detailed conversation, especially if you've been to some of the same places she has.

First impressions are all about going from HOW are you to WHO are you.

The last tool to help you discover the Common Point of Interest is an **inquiry about a person's name**. In addition to the importance of identifying, amplifying and remembering a person's name, asking about the name itself will make you UNFORGETTABLE™ every time.

Have you ever had a conversation that began about someone's name, but continued about their name for a few minutes? It's great when this happens! And you can be certain the other people are enjoying the conversation because it's all about them!

Once after giving a speech, a member of the audience approached me and introduced herself as Hannah. To find out if it was a *palindrome*, I inquired about the spelling. When she handed me her business card, immediately her name struck a chord in me because one of my favorite books as a child was called *Hannah Is a Palindrome*. This book was about a young girl in third grade named Hannah whose classmates started to make fun of her because the teacher informed the class that "Hannah" was a palindrome.

"Ha ha! Hannah is a palindrome, Hannah is a palindrome! Nah, nah, n-na nya!" they said.

Hannah, of course, was devastated.

But when the teacher explained to the students that a *palindrome* was a word that could be spelled forward and backwards, a long "ooooh" came over the students. After that, everyone loved Hannah! And all the kids were envious of her special name.

This was the story I told to Hannah, the audience member. To my surprise, she'd read the book before! We talked all about nicknames, palindromes, children's books and more. Simply because the conversation revolved around one topic: her name.

Let me ask you this...
When was the last time you inquired about somone's name?

ESSENTIAL ELEMENT FOR FLAWLESS FIRST IMPRESSIONS #5
IT'S ALL ABOUT THEM

Now that you've learned how to discover the Common Point of Interest, it's time to move into more emotional areas of first impressions. Every interaction and encounter emotionally affects both parties in some way:

- How you feel about yourself
- How you feel about others
- How others feel about you
- How others feel about themselves

In order to make an UNFORGETTABLE™ first impression (not just a *good* first impression), you must focus on the last of these emotions: **how others feel about themselves.**

> *"The great gift of conversation lies less in displaying it ourselves than in drawing it out of others. He who leaves your company pleased with himself and his own cleverness is perfectly well pleased with you."*
> JEAN DE LA BRUYERE

To solidify this element, ask yourself the following questions. If you can answer them while connecting with new people, you will be certain to become the epitome of approachability.

Does he feel like he already knows you? If you ever hear some-one say, "God I feel like we've known each other for years!" or "We really seemed to hit it off!" you're on the right track.

But you can't get to this point in the conversation without self-disclo-sure. Self-disclosure is the process of making yourself manifest to another. It starts with little pieces of information (like your name), but as you dis-cover the Common Point of Interest and share your opinions and attitudes, you will find the other person will reciprocate the same back to you. This **norm of reciprocity** is another way of saying, "I'll show you mine if you show me yours."

For example, think back to the "cereal encounter" with my friend Mitch. After I offered the question, each person sitting at the table began exchanged opinions about cereal. And after a while, the conversation reached new heights! We talked about our childhoods and other person-al stories, all of which were comfortably reciprocated among new acquaintances.

But be careful here. Say the wrong thing and you might hear one of the most annoying, overused clichés of the past 10 years come out of your conversation partner's mouth: **"TMI: Too Much Information!"** As frus-trating as this ridiculous catch phrase may be, if someone utters it, you've obviously crossed the line. Sometimes you may be several miles past the line. So be liberal with the amount of information you reveal. But be sure your level of intimacy matches that of the other person. You'll have no problem connecting with someone as if you feel like you already know each other.

How engaged is the other person? Remember this: *two monologues do not make a dialogue.* Some people just yap back and forth without engag-ing the other person like they're talking to a wall. So, be sure to incorpo-rate all parties. An important phrase you can use to assure that your dia-logue does this is: "What about you?" This sentence is the epitome **Essential Element #5: It's All About Them**.

It also allows you to turn the tables, stop talking and find out what *they're* thinking. If you reciprocate back and forth and keep both parties engaged, you will become UNFORGETTABLE™.

Are they uncertain? A common reason we feel *uncertain* during the limited first impression window is because we've forgotten names. (Think back to my mistake with Stacey/Lauren.)

Here's a hint: ASSUME people forgot your name, and then provide them with some help accordingly. First of all, wear your nametag – and wear it **easy to see**. This gives people a free opportunity to learn, or re-learn your name.

Secondly, practice the "Third Person Trick." This involves telling a story or an anecdote about yourself to help others with your name without them suffering a loss of face.

For example:

> *"...so when the airport security said, 'Scott Ginsberg,*
> *please report to the men's room for a body cavity search,'*
> *I knew I was in trouble."*

With this trick, your conversation partner will silently think to him-self, *"Oh thank God he just told me his name again – I didn't want to ask!"*

Works every time!

Has the other person discovered how similar they are to you yet? As soon as possible, find out how you are similar to your conversation partners. And make sure THEY know there's something similar. This allows you to focus on how they feel about themselves. As Napoleon Hill said, "You are a human magnet and you are constantly attracting people whose characteristics harmonize with your own."

Are you satisfying their need to feel appreciated? The number one hierarchical need of humans is the need to feel appreciated and includ-ed – and it's your job in every conversation, interaction and first impres-sion to satisfy this need. Once during an overnight shift at the Ritz Carlton in St. Louis, several gentlemen asked me to call them a cab downtown. As we waited at the front drive for the taxi to arrive, one of them asked, "So, Scott, got anyone special staying here at the Ritz tonight?"

"Sir," I smiled, "All of our guests at the Ritz Carlton are special."

The group roared in laughter! The man patted me on the shoulder and nodded his head in gratitude.

"Thanks for that Scott – that's why we love this hotel!"

Maintaining a mindset of "It's All About Them" is essential for UNFORGETTABLE™ first impressions. If you ask and answer these ques-tions, you and your conversation partners will feel like you've known each other for years. What's more, you'll make them feel appreciated, superior and comfortable while interacting with you.

ESSENTIAL ELEMENT FOR FLAWLESS FIRST IMPRESSIONS #6
BE A SOCIAL GIFT GIVER

Do you ever wonder why single people give flowers, wine, candy or mix CD's on first dates?

Bingo! Because they want to get lucky!

Just kidding. They bring gifts because they want make a great first impression. And that's the sixth and last element of this system: **giving gifts**. But I'm not talking about gifts you eat, drink, listen to or have to water. I'm talking about *social gifts*. I purposely placed this element last in the system because it helps you put into practice many of the ideas we've already covered.

In all of my reading and research on first impressions, the best description of "social gifts" was written in a book called *First Impressions* by Dr. Ann Demaris and Dr. Valerie White.[1] I'd like to look at their theory of the four types of social gifts, but take it a step further with some specific examples you can use *tomorrow* to make flawless first impressions.

Social Gift #1: Show Appreciation and Respect. Every person has some handle by which he can be lifted. As such, the two most effective ways to grab hold are with compliments and thank you's. Since we've already covered the former, let's talk about thank you's. Whenever you want to show your gratitude for something or someone, always tell people what you're thanking them for. Remember, it's the part of the blanket that hangs over the bed that keeps us warm. You will be amazed at how effective a specific thank you is:

"Thanks for your honesty; it means a lot to me."

*"Thanks for the interesting conversation, Randy.
I really learned a lot."*

*"Thanks for bringing me that bottle of water.
I thought I was going to choke on that piece of broccoli."*

Social Gift #2: Discover How You're Alike Anyone who grew up in the city of St. Louis will tell you St. Louisans are obsessed with one question when they meet someone for the first time: *"Where did you go to high school?"*

I don't know why we're obsessed with this question. But the answer always discovers the CPI (Common Point of Interest) – whether it's a per-

[1] *First Impressions.* Demasris, White

son you both know, an old football game or just a memorable teen moment. It's amazing how easy it is to give a social gift to someone simply by asking this question (And if you're reading this book and you grew up in St. Louis, my answer to "The Question" is Parkway North).

But that's a St. Louis thing. Still, the list of open ended questions you can use to find out how you and your conversation partner are alike is endless! (For other great questions, see Appendix A: "55 Great Questions to Ask Someone You Just Met.")

Let me ask you this...

What questionn will you ask to discover the Common Point of Interest?

Social Gift #3: Satisfy Curiosity On a daily basis, anywhere from four to six people ask me, "Scott, I just *have* to ask – why are you wearing a nametag?"

You may be wondering if, after more than four years, this question ever gets old.

Not at all.

I've always enjoyed answering this question not only because it allows me to talk about my passion, my business and the validation for my existence, but also because it empowers me to give a social gift as a result of being approachable. After all, seeing a nametag worn by a person who's NOT in a meeting or at work is awfully strange. And people just *have* to ask. People just *have* to satisfy their curiosity!

But there are many other ways to give social gifts for the sake of someone else's curiosity. My favorite is through trivia. You know those useless trivia facts found on daily calendars, candy wrappers and emails? They're not so useless after all.

In the summer of 2004 I read a sidebar in USA Today that said the following:

"Every year on the Fourth of July, Americans consume 150 million hotdogs.
If you lined up that amount of hotdogs from end to end,
they would stretch from the moon AND BACK seven times."

When I read this I was amazed. Maybe I was nauseous – I don't recall. Either way, I learned a piece of trivia that was both relevant AND interesting. So for the next few weeks before, during, and after the Fourth of July, I made it a point to use it at the beginning of every conversation I had.

And as it turned out; people were more interested in wieners than I thought.

We started discussions about holidays, hotdogs, fireworks, baseball games – you name it! And it was all because of a simple piece of trivia.

Here are some of my favorite examples:

- *No word in the English language rhymes with mouth, orange, silver and purple.*
- *Ancient clans that wanted to get rid of unwanted members without killing them would burn their houses down – hence the phrase "to get fired."*
- *"I am" is the shortest complete sentence in the English language.*
- *The most common first name in the world in Mohammed.*
- *The most common last name in the world is Chang.*

(For dozens of other great trivia facts, see Appendix C: "Scott's List of Not So Useless Trivia You Can Use in Conversations.")

Another great benefit of trivia is it will positively affect someone's demeanor. Offer some trivia to someone and watch as she raises her eyebrows, nods her head, smiles, alters her body language and leans forward. Trivia expedites the entire communication process! And it's all because your not-so-useless social gift will make people comfortable and more willing to communicate. Satisfying curiosity will almost always produce this result.

> *"You will get good attention and people will be more*
> *inclined to listen to you if you can make a statement*
> *whereby their response is, 'No kidding!'"*
>
> GAEL BOARDMAN

Social Gift #4: Uplift Them Do you know someone who is contagious? (Not the flu.) Perhaps their smile, laughter, positive nature or love just spreads to everyone in their presence? Think about Henry the Bellman, Cherise the Waitress and Jeffrey the Salesman from Chapter 3 – all contagious people.

GOOD NEWS: You can be contagious too!

Here's how: use fun, laughter, jokes and interesting stories in your daily repertoire of giving social gifts.

"But Scott, I can't remember any of them. I hear a joke or a story and then never think about it again."

No worries. The best way to organize this content is with a "Laughter Log." I've been using mine for several years as a way to organize my content for books, speeches, articles and learning tools. But it's also perfect for conversations. Simply get a blank notebook or journal and take a few minutes at the end of each day to write down a few notes.

Let me ask you this...

What happened this week that was funny, interesting or memorable?

Ask yourself this question; then scribble down a few notes about the incident. Do this every day and after a week or certainly after a month or year – you'll have some great material to incorporate into your "first impression lexicon."

Laughter Logs reminds me of the first time I met my friend Billy. I was a junior in college at Miami University. He and I were walking down the same path but not speaking, so I decided to break the silence.

"Hey man, you wanna hear a great joke?" I asked.

After I told him one of my favorite zingers, Billy introduced himself to me, and immediately we felt like we'd known each other for years! We walked further and realized we even knew some of the same students on campus. After we said goodbye and decided to meet up later in the week, Billy said, "Hey thanks again for the joke – I really needed a good laugh."

"Encourage one another – because you never know when someone is on the verge of giving up."

JIM ROHN

Here's a slightly different version of a social gift in a business environment. After I finished an especially draining speech at a local community center, I went to an Italian restaurant called Fazoli's. It wasn't crowded, so I took it upon myself to circumvent the impenetrable-wait-in-line-even-if-there-is-no-line-crowd-control-maze. But before I made my move, the man taking orders behind the counter sternly, yet jokingly said, "HEY SCOTT, I'M GONNA NEED YOU TO GO AROUND THE MAZE PLEASE."

I sensed his humor and replied back with, "Oh really? Well I'm gonna need you to step outside so I can strangle you with this velvet belt...whaddaya think about that?"

We both roared with laughter!

Then, for the first time in the history of fast food, he reached out to *shake my hand* while he welcomed me to Fazoli's. Now, this may not sound like a big deal, but to me, anyone who offers that amount of personal touch to a customer who is going to spend four dollars – and four *minutes* in his restaurant – is all right with me!

I looked at the menu and noticed the newest low-carb item: The Bacon Chicken Caesar. I ordered it only to be entertained once again by the clerk who did his best impression of Fat Bastard (from the Austin Powers movies) and said, *"Achhh...carbs are the enemy! Get in my belly!"*

We had a blast. I didn't even notice how slow the kitchen was moving until the clerk looked at my nametag and said, "HEY COME ON, SCOTT'S HUNGRY HERE – I NEED THAT SALAD PRONTO!"

"Sorry about the wait, Scott. If he doesn't get your salad out here in the next two minutes I'm gonna go back there and crack him over the head with this tray."

Wow. Talk about friendly service...not counting the pending violent attack on his coworker.

"Here you go Scott, enjoy. And thanks for coming into Fazoli's!"

Now, earlier in our conversation I overheard one of his managers using his name, so I said, "And thank you...*Dustin*."

"Hey, how the heck did you know *my* name?!" Dustin asked.

As I headed out the door, Low Carb Bacon Chicken Caesar in hand, I said "What goes around comes around my friend!"

POWER PRINCIPLE #4
BEING APPROACHABLE MEANS FRIENDLY AND READY TO LISTEN AND HELP

I don't need to tell you how important first impressions are. You know they have long lasting power and you know there's limited time to make them. The point of this system is:

Everyone else in the world is trying to make a good first impression – but good doesn't cut it anymore.

If you want to become the epitome of approachability, you need to be UNFORGETTABLE™! As we come to the end of these two chapters, let's review the second three Essential Elements for Flawless First Impressions.

Discover the CPI (Common Point of Interest) – find common ground as soon as possible

It's All About Them – be sure to focus on how other people feel about themselves

Become a Social Gift Giver – show appreciation, find out how you're alike, satisfy curiosity and uplift people with humor

CHAPTER FIVE

Become a Great Conversationalist

Effectively Engaging in Every Encounter

"Humans have already changed the world several times by changing the way they have had conversations."

THEODORE ZELDIN

CONVERSATIONS CREATE OUR WORLD. THINK ABOUT THE LAST TIME YOU HAD ONE of those incredibly engaging, incredibly enriching conversations. Maybe it was with an old friend. Perhaps it was with a coworker. Maybe it was a random person in line at the store!

Notwithstanding the context or level of your encounters, one simple fact is true: **the human soul is incomplete without conversation.** Yes, it is always an experiment where the results are never guaranteed. Yes, it involves risk. But when you take that first step to move beyond "How are you?" and "Can you believe it snowed again?" it will propel you past the clichés and into more valuable territory.

Conversation is a basic human need. Without it, humans go crazy! As such, you must regard its daily consumption to be as healthy as food, water and exercise. In fact, the need for social contact is so fundamental, it is biologically based:

Socially connected people who have frequent interactions with friends and family are less prone to stress.

I once gave a speech when a member of the audience told this story about how to start conversations with new people.

"My friend and I were on a ski trip a few years ago. Our lift up the mountain took about 15 minutes, so he decided to talk to the other person on the lift. He noticed the other man's nametag, so he said, 'Good morning Brad, how are you?'

The other man grinned as they began to talk for about 15 minutes. It turned out Brad was a ski instructor! He gave us all kinds of tips and tricks for getting down the mountain successfully.

When we approached the end of the lift, the three of us got onto the mountain, and Brad the Instructor said, 'Nice talking with you guys. And hey, you just got a free $50 ski lesson!'"

Let me ask you this...

What could you learn by starting a conversation with one new person a day?

Every successful conversation adds strength to our sense of community and instills a feeling of belonging. *Social capital* is a term defined by Robert Putnam[1] as "your reserve of personal bonds and fellowship." Old friends, a family member, an authority figure, a church leader or a complete stranger – these are the individuals who have the most resonance in our lives. And there is nothing more cathartic than to walk away from someone whose words made you feel alive. After such encounters, you will never be the same person again.

Conversation is, according to Theodore Zeldin, "An adventure in which we agree to cook the world together to make it taste less bitter." However, it cannot begin until you are willing to take that pivotal first step – and without our interpersonal courage; conversation cannot continue. In this chapter, we'll examine several keys for becoming a great conversationalist:

- Tips for Talking Like a Pro

- How to Avoid Falling Asleep Behind the Conversational Wheel

- Using Flavored Answers in Conversation

- What to Do When You Can't Remember Someone

[1] *Bowling Alone*, Putnam

> # POWER PRINCIPLE #5
> # BEING APPROACHABLE MEANS EASY TO MEET, CONVERSE AND DO BUSINESS WITH

TIPS FOR TALKING LIKE A PRO

According to the World Psychological Association, six out of every ten people has a fear of talking to strangers. When you enter a room full of new faces, starting conversations seems like an impossible task. You wait and wait and hope to God someone else says hello first, but the apprehensive silence persists. Then nobody talks to anybody.

This unwillingness to communicate will result in missed opportunities to meet new friends and make mutually valuable connections. And although your initial timidity takes time and practice to overcome, **the more often you throw yourself into the sea, the less likely the waves are to bother you.** That's the nature of approachability.

They won't say hello back to me. They won't be interested in me. I will make a fool of myself.

Thoughts like these are the reason we have difficulty starting conversations. But the more often you start conversations, the better you will become at it. So, be the first to introduce yourself or say hello. And when you take an *active* instead of a *passive* role, your skills will develop and there will be less chance for rejection. Also understand the gains vs. losses. After all, what's so bad about being rejected by someone you don't even know?

During my research for this book, I received an email with an attached article about two New Yorkers named Liz and Bill.[2] They start conversations with one of the most creative front porches I've ever heard of! They stand around in New York City all day, every day with a two-foot tall sign out on the sidewalk that reads "TALK TO ME." On a daily basis, the scene is packed with customers and conversationalists who

[2] www.nyctalktome.com

bring up just about any topic one could imagine! They do this anywhere from 8 to 14 hours a day, travel on foot from neighborhood to neighborhood across the five boroughs, camping out in various areas. In the win-

ter, their territory includes warmer locations such as bars, clubs, coffee shops, subway stations and hotels.

According to Liz and Bill, they do this because they feel people need to talk to each other. Their actions contain no hidden motive – just plain, old-fashioned, friendly conversation.

"Strangers have a lot to teach each other in ways they could never imagine," said Bill. "And this city needs a place to trade and experience the thousands of diverse ideas and perspectives New Yorkers carry around with them."

Bill and Liz's sign is a perfect example of how to use a **front porch** to start conversations and invite people into your world. But, because approachability is a two way street and equally dedicated to developing the confidence to talk to someone else, let's look at another great technique for stepping onto someone *else's* front porch in conversation.

My friend Greg once told me his favorite technique to start and maintain conversations:

"I write geography software which I sell to schools around the USA. I have used the software to learn names of most countries of the world. I know a few facts about each country – only where it is located and perhaps the shape of the country.

But, when I see someone or hear someone who I think might be from a foreign country, I simply smile and ask them, 'Where are you from?' When they tell me where they are from, I simply say (for example) 'Oh, yes, the Gambia is on the northwest edge of Africa – surrounded by Senegal – and the Gambia river runs through it.'

That's all it takes! Most foreigners (or immigrants who have lived in the USA for decades) are so shocked that an American knows anything about geography, they break into a big smile and a conversation begins!

I believe knowledge of geography can help bring us toward world peace because it is harder to hate people if we know something about them."

Let me ask you this...
What unique knowledge, information or experiences could you use to spice up your conversations?

Here's another tip for talking like a pro: **avoid the weather**. Because I once lived in Portland, Oregon where it rained 300 days of the year, I never complained about the weather. Another reason I didn't complain about the weather is because, without it, 90% of the world wouldn't know how to start a conversation!

In fact, I've read almost every book on how to start conversations, mingling, breaking the ice and meeting people – and I have yet to find one that doesn't advise the following:

> "Talking about the weather is an easy and
> effective way to start a conversation."

No it isn't. It's a terrible way. And just because it's easy and everyone uses it doesn't make it effective. Starting a conversation about the weather actually means you've *settled* for starting a conversation about the weather; which makes your conversation partners feel like you've *settled* for them too. Every time you do it, you also show the other person you aren't a good enough conversationalist to talk about anything other than the weather. So, unless there's a good reason such as a tornado, hailstorm, tsunami, meteor shower or lightning happened to strike your cat – think of something else. You can do better than that.

BUT WHAT DO I SAY?

OK, you're not sure *what* to talk about? No worries. Here are a few suggestions of where to get your material:

- **Read.** Newspapers, magazines and other publications are a wealth of interesting, funny or useful tidbits to use in your conversations. I recommend subscribing to several daily or weekly email lists such as Yahoo! Groups, various ezines[3], newsletters and daily tips to keep your mind full of new topics. You will be surprised how much useful information you can learn!

- **Write.** You don't have to be a writer to write. Keep a journal of interesting stories, events, thoughts and jokes you've experienced. Organize your thoughts. Update it regularly and look at it often. After a few months – even weeks – the writing will accumulate and you'll never be short of things to say!

- **Think Ahead.** If you're going to an event, club, restaurant, or place of business, go to their website before you walk in the door. This will provide useful fodder for your conversations, not to mention driving maps for the directionally challenged (i.e., me). Most how-to articles and books on interviewing skills will give you this same advice. But don't limit conversational preparation just for job interviews. Believe it or not, your performance in every conversation is evaluated in some way.

...AND HOW DO I SAY IT?

It's easy to walk into a room full of new faces and think: *"All of these people are strangers. I came into the conversation too late. I'm not sure how to get involved with the discussion."*

Thoughts like these are soaked with uncertainty, and the simplest way to reduce that is to be an active listener. Make eye contact with the person speaking. And, keep your ears open for **iceberg statements.** These are pieces of free information where ninety percent is under the surface waiting to be talked about. For example, listen for an implied statement about someone's family or other key phrases/hot buttons. These will help you discover the CPI (Common Point of Interest.) Be sure to smile, nod and respond with follow up inquiries. This allows you to become included as a part of the conversation.

Also, don't forget the value of **eye contact.** It is the single most effective indicator that conversation is desirable. When you avoid it, you will be perceived as anxious, uninterested and bored with the conversation and the company. As a matter of fact, to start a conversation with a person whose eyes are fixed on the ground is about as easy as hurdling *over* that person!

---

[3] I recommend the *Building Front Porches Ezine* at www.hellomynameisscott.com

Think of it this way: **why do lights always reside at the highest part of the elevator door?** So you don't have to talk to the person next to you! You gaze at the beautiful yellow numbers ascending to the penthouse while your conversation plummets to the basement!

When your eyes are focused up, down, away, at your watch, at your notes or simply off into space, nobody is going to talk to you. Tom Robbins described it best in *Even Cowgirls Get the Blues* when he said: "Like a reclusive movie actress, she donned a scarf and dark glasses and studied her walking feet as if she had a research grant from the stubbed toe foundation." Remember, eyes always talk. And they always provide valuable cues for approachability.

Another common vehicle for this expression is through **hand and arm placement.** As the old saying goes, "You cannot say nothing." Nonverbal communication expresses emotion, conveys attitude and communicates your personal traits more than any language in the world!

Here's a tip: don't place your hands over your face, mouth or anywhere close to your head. If you bite your nails, play with your hair or tap your fingers against your mouth, forget about it! People will assume you're engrossed in deep thought and unavailable for conversation.

Also beware of the most common, most physical nonverbal barrier: **crossing your arms.** Even if you're cold, don't do it. Nobody will want to "bother" you. They will form the impression you are defensive, nervous, judgmental, close minded or skeptical. They will also form the impression that you're **not** approachable.

Let me ask you this...

Would you approach someone whose arms were crossed?

Talking like a pro also involves avoiding **behaviors that close you off**. Think about this: why do people read the paper, listen to headphones or talk on their cell phones in public? To catch up on the news, relax and stay in contact with each other? Maybe. But these types of barriers decrease approachability and result in missed opportunities to create connections.

When you use something to protect yourself from involvement with people, knowingly or not, you put up a nonverbal barrier. These barriers tell others two things: 1) you're busy, and 2) to start a conversation with you will be an exercise in futility.

But with proper hand, arm and body position, you appear open and ready to talk. With proper eye contact and a contagious smile, you come off as friendly and polite. And, with a continual desire to break the silence without shielding yourself from interaction, others will be happy to step onto your front porch!

Now that you've learned a few tips for talking like a pro, let's move into the next section: How to Avoid Falling Asleep Behind the Conversational Wheel.

HOW TO AVOID FALLING ASLEEP BEHIND THE CONVERSATIONAL WHEEL

I once had an unfortunate encounter with road rage on Highway 72 driving from St. Louis to Moline, Illinois. I was scheduled to give the keynote address to a school district in late March. During my drive up there, a large Ford truck driven by an even larger man almost caused me to crash into the median. Apparently 78 mph wasn't fast enough for him, so he decided to run me off the highway! (Only to be followed by a variety of choice phrases that weren't exactly *approachable*.)

Although my near crash *did* eliminate one of my future bathroom breaks, I still became frustrated and gave some serious thought to the problems people encounter while driving. Then I realized how similar driving was to conversation.

Think about the last time you feel asleep behind the wheel. Dangerous, wasn't it? Even if it's just for a split second, nodding off while driving puts you and the other drivers at risk.

But even when you're *not* driving, it's still possible to fall asleep behind the wheel. The *conversational* wheel, that is.

For example, how many times have you zoomed past your turn because you were uncertain where to get off? If you drive like me, this might happen to you three or four times a week. (Thanks for nothing, MapQuest.)

Similarly, when you are uncertain in conversation, you can also **miss your turn**. Here's why: uncertainty breeds from fear of rejection – the number one reason people don't start conversations. However, practice will make your fear fade away.

Try taking a more *active* role in your conversations and prepare your introduction ahead of time. Think about what you will say when you meet new people. Every time you walk into work, an event, your home or any other place in public, have three topics of discussion ready to go. Reading the newspaper or searching news online is a great way to get some good ideas.

Another effective technique is to have one or two open-ended questions ready in advance to help encourage self-disclosure and engagement. I use a new one every week!

Here are a few great examples:

- *Do you go by a nickname?*
- *Who is the most famous person you've ever met?*
- *What's your favorite childhood TV show?*
- *What is your favorite daily ritual?*
- *What was the best concert you ever attended?*
- *What is the best book you've read about your field?*
- *If you could memorize any book cover to cover, which one would it be?*
- *If you could hear anyone in history give a speech, whom would you hear?*

(Read dozens of other questions just like these in Appendix A: "55 Great Questions to Ask Someone You Just Met.")

Keep Your Eyes on the Road

One of these days my CD player is going to get me into an accident. I'm always distracted by that darn thing!

When interacting with people, what distracts you? Other stuff on your mind? Other people to talk to? Too self-conscious? Think about the last time you were introduced to someone and forgot everything about him or her. Especially his or her name. Ouch! The reason you forgot so quickly is because you were distracted. You didn't take a genuine interest other others because you were too busy thinking about *you*.

In conversation, you're #2...they are #1

Conversation, just like driving, requires focus. Stay in tune to the moment of people's introduction and repeat back key information you just heard. "That's interesting *Elena*, I didn't know Monsanto was expanding." This will widen the areas of your memory circuit and make it easier to connect and communicate with people around you. Remember, it's more valuable to concentrate on the *road* than the *soundtrack to* the road.

Don't Swerve into the Wrong Lane

Isn't it frustrating when someone veers into your lane without a signal? It's almost as if she's invaded your personal space!

Conversation is the same way: you must respect personal space. Most social contexts adhere to the same spatial principles: 18 inches for intimate distance; 3 feet for personal distance; and 4-12 feet for social distance.

Remember *The Hero* personality type from Chapter 1 – the host/flight attendant who burst my interpersonal bubble and poked the nametag on my chest? Perfect example. **Don't do this.** People value their personal space.

If you'd like to approach others who are engaged in conversation, examine their "lane" before you think it's safe to merge. And when the time is right to join in the conversation, always remember to use nonverbal listening cues like nodding and eye contact; ask open ended questions based on iceberg statements or politely add an opinion or observation to show your desire to be included. Try this, and they will be happy to let you into their conversation!

Don't Promote Road Rage

Imagine some guy in the lane next to you who won't give you space to turn. His music is blasting. He's way over the speed limit. And he doesn't care one bit about where you had to be 10 minutes ago! This is a typical example of a situation that elicits **road rage.**

Did you know the term *road rage* is in the dictionary? It's defined as "anger or violence between drivers, often caused by difficult driving conditions." But people just *love* to blame traffic for driving conditions – not their own unapproachable behaviors – for this level of discomfort and uncertainty.

Now think about the last meeting, event or party you attended.

While driving down the road of social interaction, did you elicit road rage from other drivers? Were you unapproachable? Did you avoid eye contact? Did you forget names? Perhaps it wasn't the traffic after all.

The average American spends 72 minutes in his or her car every day. Although getting from Point A to Point B is necessary to maintain your daily routine, never forget:

The most important trip of your day is on the road of social interaction.

Therefore, in order to drive safely and avoid falling asleep behind the conversational wheel, adhere to the following rules:

- *Don't miss your turn:* be aware of oncoming opportunities to make valuable connections
- *Keep your eyes on the road:* focus on the moment of introduction to maintain rapport with people you've just met
- *Don't swerve into the wrong lane:* offer open, nonverbal signals to those with whom you want to communicate
- *Don't promote road rage:* make certain other people are comfortable in your presence.

DON'T I KNOW YOU FROM SOMEWHERE?

I publish an ezine called *Building Front Porches*, a free newsletter that goes out to thousands of subscribers around the world who want to become more effective, engaging communicators. Every other week, I run an article from my column, inspirational stories, resources and responses to "Ask the Expert Questions." In one of the 2003 issues, I was asked this question:

Dear Scott:

What do you do if you notice, or are talking to someone you SHOULD know, but for one reason or another can't remember?

Let me discuss the answer to this important question in this section by giving some tips for solving this conversational mystery. Picture this:

You see her from across the room. You know her, but you can't remember how you know her. Now you have a problem: you want to break the ice but your uncertainty is holding you back. Uh oh, she's heading in your direction. What do you do?!

If you've ever been in this situation before, you know how uncomfortable it can get – especially if you *really should* know who the person is. What's more, it's not uncommon to evade those whom you cannot remember for the fear of embarrassment.

People forget people everyday. But the right attitude, questioning, conversational direction and communication tools will help you pinpoint whom you're talking to. Let's examine some techniques to do so without risking total embarrassment while still maintaining your approachability.

Like every other skill in the world, this too starts with **attitude.** Don't worry that you have no idea who the heck you're talking to. Empty your mind of distracting thoughts like, "This guy's office has been down the hall from mine for 11 years," or "How could I forget her name? She's my sister!" These self-loathing thoughts will impede you from actively listening to what people are saying, the contents of which will potentially contain valuable clues.

And don't feel bad when you blank on someone's name, occupation or the time when you first met. Everyone's been there before. It's not the end of the world.

The easiest and most gracious technique to find out how you know someone is **honesty.** It's always the best policy. Now obviously, the willingness to admit you've forgotten something – or in this case, someone – is not an easy thing to do. In fact, sometimes it's downright humiliating! But honesty is the quickest way to solve a conversational mystery. So, if you don't have a problem flat-out telling people you can't remember who they are or how you know them, here's how to **take one for the team.**

First and foremost, DON'T say the word "forget." It will only make someone feel unimportant. It's less offensive when you use polite verbiage to downplay the idea of "forgetting" with such phrases as "Please remind me," "Could you help me with," "I'm terrible with remembering" and "It slipped my mind." People will be glad to offer the information you have misplaced in exchange for you admittance of a temporary brain poof.

Here's another effective tool for figuring out who certain people are:

If you want to learn information about the person you're talking to, open up. Your _ears_, that is.

The trick is to listen for **iceberg statements.** As you've already learned, these are key words, phrases or sentences under which 90% of the important information awaits your discovery. But be patient. And as soon as you hear an iceberg statement, follow it up with an open ended question to dive beneath the surface. In time, what you need to remember about someone will be revealed to you.

Now, let's say you're already engaging with someone, but you can't remember who she is. And, you aren't comfortable admitting your memory lapse. In this situation, the most effective technique is to **ask open ended questions to encourage people to disclose who they are**. This front porch behavior will empower them to open up and something will jar your memory.

For example, imagine you can't remember where Erin works. Simply ask her questions that allude to general scheduling like, "What's on tap for this week?" or "What projects are keeping you busy?" Another great topic bound to narrow down job possibilities is travel: "Any trips or travel plans coming up?" Lastly, asking people "Who are you here with?" is a perfect way to jar your memory.

This reminds me of a classic episode of *Seinfeld*. Jerry was unsure of a certain woman's name. During their conversation he told a story about various nicknames he had as a kid. Then he asked her if she had any nicknames. Even though poor Jerry never *did* get her name until the credits rolled, this was a great example (albeit an over exaggerated one) of how self-disclosure provides an outlet through which one party will reveal the exact same information so desperately needed by the other.

Whatever you want to learn about someone, start by telling him that same fact about yourself.

Another excellent tip for finding out whom you're talking to when you have no idea whom you're talking to is **introducing a third party**. Almost every book on how to remember names, faces and people and the like will tell you to use this technique. And it works just about every time.

If you can't place a person's name, position, company, family, this technique uses your socializing skills to bring two new people together. Tell the person whose information you've misplaced, "I'd like you to meet a friend of mine." Grab your friend and say, "This is Gary, he and I work together at Amcorp." (Before you do this, signal or whisper to Gary you need his help with the other person's information.) Gary, being the polite conversationalist he is, will elicit an introduction and a conversation to eventually draw out the information you need.

Now, if someone across the room catches your eye but you can't seem to remember her, third parties are perfect for pre-conversation preparation. Before stepping on the front porch of the pseudo-stranger, find someone else you KNOW and ask him or her all about your forgotten friend. With a few simple questions, you will easily gain the knowledge to become more approachable so you can connect and communicate with anybody – even the people you forgot.

Finally, if you ever reach a point in the conversation where you don't feel comfortable admitting you forgot someone, can't think of any open ended questions or don't have access to a third party, there are always **props,** i.e., front porch objects. The most effective prop is someone's business card. It contains all the pertinent names, logos, websites and other visual "Ah ha's!" to lubricate the hamster wheel known as your brain. But don't tell her you lost her card – that's just as bad as saying you "forgot" her name. Simply request another card and quickly glace at it while you thank her and put it in your pocket.

Depending on where you're having a conversation, dozens of other props are useful to jar your memory as well: nametags, promotional items, briefcases, table tents and the like. Props are incredibly effective because *people remember that which appeals to their visual sense three times more than the other senses.*

But whatever technique you use to discover *who* the person is you're talking to, remember this: **the longer you interact without knowing who you're talking to, the more uncomfortable you will become**. Uncertainty is a communication barrier that hinders approachability, and the only way to reduce it is to identify and extract information about people. Use the techniques of questioning, free information, third parties, props and active listening. (If all else fails, just admit you've suffered a memory lapse!) And with practice and the right attitude, you'll never have to say "There goes what's-her-name from that thing with the guy at the place" again.

USING FLAVORED ANSWERS IN CONVERSATIONS

In Chapter 3 you learned how to turn water into lemonade by giving flavored answers to fruitless questions like "How are you?" "What's up?" and "How's it going?" This technique does more than create UNFORGETTABLE™ first impressions; it empowers people to enhance an otherwise mundane conversation, so let's close this chapter by using what we've learned so far and take it to the next level.

In order to create your own flavored answers, they must have a mixture of the right ingredients. These characteristics of flavored answers will lay a foundation from which you can create your own flavor. Read these, and soon you will be turning water into lemonade with only a few words!

Flavored Means Original

Become known for the way you answer mundane questions with something unique and creative. When I saw George Carlin in concert in Toledo, OH in 2001, he told the audience this: "I hate answering the same stupid, mundane questions in the same, stupid way. I've decided I will use a new adjective every month just to keep my answers fresh. This month, I'm ubiquitous."

Flavored Means A Personification of Your Attitude

People can learn a great deal about your attitudes and values simply by the way you reply to "How are you doing?" What's more, flavored answers to fruitless questions are **self-fulfilling prophecies:** tell someone you're "On top of the world," and you just might find yourself there.

Flavored Means Surprising

Say something completely unexpected. Even say the exact opposite of what the person expects to hear. Several years ago I was wearing a Michigan Football hat the day after Ohio State demolished them 49-10. A man wearing an Ohio State jersey approached me, rudely got in my face and with an arrogant smirk and said, "Hey man – did you see the Ohio State/Michigan game last night?!"

"No, I don't really care about sports," I said. (This is true.)

He was silenced. Dumbfounded. A complete a loss for words! I smiled back and he ended up changing the subject after which we had a friendly conversation.

Flavored Means Memorable

Use words that differentiate you. Millions of conversations take place every minute. So, what can you say that resonates in someone's heart that he hasn't already heard 20 times today? Once during a speech to a healthcare marketing association, I told the audience to respond to a question in unison. I asked, "I want everyone to shout out their answer to this question: 'How are you?'"

In perfect harmony, 199 audience members muttered, "Fine."

And one man sitting directly to my left bellowed, "Grrrrreat!!"

It was beautiful. I'll never forget it. And neither will those other 199 people who didn't give a flavored answer – (I stopped the speech and gave the man a free copy of one of my books!)

Flavored Means Honest and Open

We are afraid to disclose the way we really feel in response to mundane, ritual questions because there's limited time to do so. What's more, revealing emotions doesn't seem worth it. Unfortunately, this isn't conducive to flow in our conversations.

On the other hand, when someone willingly gives themselves to you in an honest and open way, he truly becomes a great conversationalist! I'll never forget the time I asked an elderly man, "How are you?" to which he replied, "I'm old, I'm Italian, and I'm rich!" Talk about honest and open!

Ok, now that you've got some ideas of flavored answers to give to fruitless, mundane questions – let's explore the value. Whether you're with a customer, making a new friend, on a date or networking with colleagues, here is what you (and your conversation partner) will experience when you offer flavored answers to fruitless questions.

YOUR ANSWER WILL...

- **Show someone you care.** This is undoubtedly the most important virtue of communication. The openness and honesty of your flavored answer will show someone you value the conversation, and therefore, her as a person.
- **Build trust.** Self-disclosure is reciprocal proportionate to the amount of information you reveal. Whether you're attending a sales meeting, on a date or joining a club, give part of yourself to the other person immediately. He will do the same, and as a result you will feel like you've known each other for years!
- **Remind people that talking to you was worth it.** Have you ever left a conversation with someone and said, "Boy...I'm sure glad I got to talk to him!"? What caused you to say that? Perhaps it was their flavored answer!

- **Trigger someone's psychological need to be included.** I don't care how much of a rush, how bad of a day or how tired people are – they need be included and engage with each other. Give them an answer to make them feel appreciated.
- **Magnetize people to you.** Think back to Henry the Bellman from Chapter 3. When I asked him "How are you?" he responded, "Everything is beautiful!" How could anyone hear those words and not be completely drawn to the person who said it?

Every time someone asks a fruitless question like "How are you?" "What's up?" or "How's business?" he expects to hear you say "fine." He expects to have his level of conversational depth reciprocated.

But when you give a surprising, honest, appealing, memorable and fun answer that personifies your attitude, it will expedite the interaction and create an engaging conversation. People will walk away from you thinking, "Wow! What a great conversationalist!"

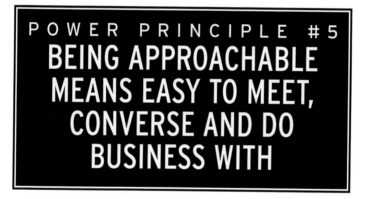

POWER PRINCIPLE #5
BEING APPROACHABLE MEANS EASY TO MEET, CONVERSE AND DO BUSINESS WITH

CHAPTER SIX

Drop Me A Line

Communicating Effectively via Email and Phone

*"Every technological advance is one step
forward for convenience, but one step back for relationships."*

DAVID RICH

IMAGINE YOU JUST FINISHED TALKING TO A FRIEND OR CLIENT FROM ACROSS THE country. As you hang up, you hold your cell phone in the palm of your hand; shake your head in amazement and wonder: How the heck did we get by without these things?

Now picture yourself sitting at a booth at a coffee shop, pounding away on your laptop. You're connected through a high speed wireless network, emailing people around the world while getting the latest news from CNN.com. And you say: *What ever happened to dial up modems?*

The acceleration of our technology is scary. This is a good and a bad thing. It's *good* scary because we are able to communicate with each other around the world instantly via media never before conceived by man. And it's *bad* scary, because we have become so dependent on technology that we now use it to communicate in a manner that's unfriendly and unapproachable. This is likely to further isolate us from the same people with whom we are trying to connect.

The key to finding balance between technology and face to face communication is to communicate *electronically* in a similar way you communicate *interpersonally:* by using the power of approachability.

POWER PRINCIPLE #6
BEING APPROACHABLE
MEANS CAPABILITY OF
BEING REACHED

In this chapter, we're going to concentrate on the two forms of communication used most frequently, yet suffer from the most deficiencies: **email** and **phone.**

PART 1: EMAIL APPROACHABILITY

Think of the last time you received an email from someone, read it, and said to yourself, "Boy was that a lifeless, ill-prepared, impersonal message – looks like Randy *really* cared to stay connected with me!"

You don't want to be like Randy. You want to make the recipient feel like you're right there next to him. You want someone to be excited when he or she receives an email from you. And you want to reassure people email *can* be personable, Viagra spam notwithstanding. But because email is one of the major media of business and personal communication, you must treat it with the same level of personality you hope to convey through daily, face to face interactions. In other words, **think of your emails as real conversations and you will elicit real connections.**

Write Conversationally

No email will ever beat face to face interaction. But you *do* enhance the level of friendliness if you write in a conversational tone. Use simple words. They sound genuine. Don't try to impress someone by thesaurusizing your email with terms you wouldn't use in person– it sounds diaphanous and supercilious.

Also, don't be afraid to use one or two word sentences. After all, you use them every day in your face to face conversations – so why is email any different? I suggest exclamations like "Wow!" and "That's great!" People will truly appreciate it when you create a memorable presence.

A great acid test for this is to read every email aloud before you send it. When you finish, ask yourself this question:

Does my email make it sound like I am personally engaging with the recipient?

Use *Italics*, **Boldface** and **Punctuation!**

One of the pitfalls of email is its inability to convey emotion. Often your correspondent won't understand if you are serious or kidding, happy or sad, frustrated or euphoric – unless you are *expressive*. Punctuation, sentence structure, paragraph separation and grammar are rules people seem to forget when writing emails. So use *italics* to highlight key words to show the person exactly what you want to say. Otherwise, your opinions, statements and stories will be misinterpreted. (The same goes for **boldface** words.)

Subject Headings

If there's ever a place in your email to add personality, it's the subject heading. After all, most businesspeople get dozens of emails a day – so what could you do to entice them to read yours first? It's almost like the first impression of your email. Have fun with it! Put something to grab attention like a joke, quotation or interesting phrase. You have plenty of room too – usually up to 50 characters – so don't be afraid to fill up the space.

One of my favorite subject headings is to pose a question related to the body text such as "Why don't people talk in elevators?" or "Did you see that game yesterday?" Just like your face to face conversations, the difference between a boring and exciting subject heading is all about engagement, i.e., "Hey" vs. "Wait until you hear about my weekend…"

Keeping Up

Here's an important question to consider: Do you check your phone messages every day? Or do you let that blinking red light pulsate out of the corner of your eye for a week before you listen to the recording and call someone back?

Of course you listen to your phone messages every day! Why wouldn't you? Besides, there's bound to be some important calls on there you'd like to return immediately.

OK, so let me ask you this: When you're at work, do you look at new papers in your box consistently? Or do you let that bundle of folders, papers and flyers spew out of edge onto the floor?

Of course you check your mail often! You don't want to miss any important dates or notes.

And yet, some businesspeople don't check their email every day. Why not? How is email any less important as a form of communication? There's no reason to check email with less frequency than any other medium. As a matter of fact, email has an immediacy that *requires* a quicker response than older forms of communication.

Let me ask you this…

How many times a day do you check and reply to emails?

Handle the Overload

Have you ever received an email that bombarded you with seven or eight questions, one after another? Letters like these are tough to reply to unless you organize your response. The best way to handle the overload is through the following reply process:

- Start a blank email, either a reply or a new message.

- Offer an introductory paragraph to thank the person for his or her questions and tell him or her that the answers are organized below.

- Go through the body text of the original email and locate each of the questions.

- Cut, copy and paste each question in the blank space of the new letter as a subheading for your response. (It helps to italicize or bold the original question.)

- Under each question, give your response.

- Offer a closing paragraph and your signature.

Signature

Whatever program you use for email – Outlook, Eudora, Yahoo, Hotmail – find out how to customize your signature. There's nothing more frustrating than receiving an email from someone who wants to talk further, get together or have you send her something, *that doesn't have any personal information in the email*. At the end of every email you send, always **cross reference** the following information:
- Name
- Title
- Company/Organization
- Mailing address
- At least two phone numbers
- Fax number
- Email address
- Website
- A few sentences about yourself, your company or your job

Think of it this way: Have you ever received a handwritten letter from someone that had no return address stamped on the envelope?

(This also makes it less likely that your email will end up as automatic junk or spam.)

The way you write and send your email personifies your attitude, values and interpersonal effectiveness. Unfortunately, friendliness and engagement are the things we sacrifice for technological speed and efficiency. But just because email is faster, doesn't mean it has to be less friendly. And just because email is sent across the country, doesn't mean it can't be engaging. So remember:

An email that sounds like a person will be treated like a person.

HOW TO WRITE EMAIL INTRODUCTIONS

The purpose of an email introduction is to bring together two people you know who:

a) Should meet

b) Have something in common

c) Can help each other

d) All of the above

Because email is simply another medium of communication, you need to approach it as such. When you type out the text to an email introduction, think about the key phrases you would say **in person** when you introduce two new people.

Some tips for an effective email introduction are:

- Give a short, few sentence background on each person
- Explain your relationship with each person
- Provide phone numbers, websites and email addresses
- Keep it short, casual and friendly
- Stress the idea of "helping each other out"

Here's an example of an effective email introduction...

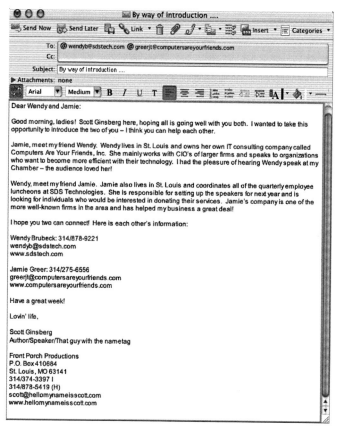

Let me ask you this...

What two people could you connect with an email introduction?

The last point about communicating effectively via email is **over usage.** Technology – because of its speed and efficiency – has a tendency to be used *too* much. It's just SO easy! (When I was in college, I used to jokingly Instant Message my roommate, Charles. It drove him crazy!)

But think about these common business situations:

- Have you ever emailed several times back and forth to someone whose cubicle/office was right behind you?
- Or sent 5 letters in one day to the same coworker down the hall?
- What about receiving an instant reply to an email 17 seconds after you just sent it?

Sometimes, it's easier to stop emailing and just pick up the phone. Or walk down the hall. Or walk down the street. Or turn your chair around and talk to the person sitting right behind you!

Try this: next time you receive an email from a customer, a boss, a friend or a complete stranger – don't email them back. Try communicating using a different, unexpected medium. Maybe, call them right back. Or show up at their office. Do a*nything* that enhances the personal connection!

This reminds me of the lovable character, Kramer from Seinfeld. Every time his neighbor, Jerry, called him on the phone, what did he do? He just walked across the hall and popped into Jerry's apartment!

Don't resign yourself to communicating in impersonal ways – pick a medium that manifests approachability and makes people feel important. And I guarantee you will absolutely blow them away with **your capability of being reached.**

PART 2: PHONE APPROACHABILITY

Even more prominent than the use of email is the one piece of technology our society could not live without: **cell phones.**

What's the first thing people do as soon as they leave a room, meeting, seminar, church, movie or concert?

No more than five years ago the answer was "talk to the other people about the event," "grab their keys," "light up a cigarette" or "walk to the car." But now, people can't walk ten yards out the door without whipping out their cell phones.

This further illustrates our society's dependence on technology to stay connected. But what people don't realize is, because of this dependence, they often practice behaviors that exacerbate their ability to communicate effectively.

In this section, we'll explore phone approachability from two sides: *cell phone* etiquette and *voicemail* effectiveness.

CELL PHONE DO'S AND DON'TS

What would we do without our cell phones? Wow, there's a scary question. It's hard to imagine a world without them. But cell phones, connected as they may keep us, seem to have an amazing power to disturb and trump face to face interaction.

For example, why is it that during a meal or a meeting, people insist on taking every call? Even worse, just let the phone ring? They forget all about the person across the table as if they he or she were invisible! This violates the golden rule of interpersonal communication, which is to make the other person feel like he or she is the most important person in the world.

But there are ways to avoid embarrassing yourself while still honoring the person across the table. (This information is NOT found in the 147 page Sprint PCS handbook.) Whether you're at lunch or in a one-on-one meeting, use the following etiquette tips to combat even the most enticing barriers that stand in your way of being an effective communicator.

DO...Be Subtle, Yet Accessible

The three possible locations to keep your phone are: bag, belt or pocket. Many people chose to keep cell phones in their bags because of pocket-less wardrobes. If this is the case for you, be sure to choose a vibrating or single beep ring that's audible, yet minimal so it doesn't ring several times while you search through your bag.

Pockets and belt clips are the most efficient places to keep your phone because you are able to answer the ringer right away. Also, it's easy to **silence the ringer** right away. Remember, the last thing your friends or colleagues want to hear during the meeting is an annoying MIDI version of Beethoven's 9th piercing their ears several times.

DO NOT...Lay Your Phone on the Table

The moment you sit down to lunch with someone, what's the first thing you do? Check out the menu? Take a sip of water? Unfold your napkin? If you're like me, you succumb to the power of the almighty carbohydrate and go to town on the rolls.

But imagine this: you sit down to eat only to watch the person across the table reach into her pocket, grab her cell phone, and smack it right down next to the salt shaker.

Ouch.

Does this mean she has an emergency call coming in? Probably not.

It sounds more like, as Seinfeld says, "I have 62 other people on speed dial I could call if I wanted to; so you better be interesting." This is not the way to make someone feel important.

Let me ask you this...

Where do you keep your cell phone during a meal?

DO...Take Emergencies

If you know ahead of time an incoming call is a business or personal emergency, answer it. This is what cell phones are for. Tell the other person ahead of time that you are expecting such a call and that's why you haven't turned the cell phone off.

But other than an emergency message or a call that directly affects all people the conversation at hand, nobody who is calling you can't wait an hour for you to call him back. Don't worry; the person calling won't get mad. In the history of cell phones, no caller has ever said, "You were in a meeting?! And THEN you decided to call me back?! How rude!"

Still, Mr. Miyagi from *The Karate Kid II* put it best when he said, "Best way to block punch – no be there." In other words, if you're in a meeting or a meal with someone else, just turn your phone off. Or don't bring it. This is a great way to avoid incoming calls or the temptation to make outgoing calls while still maintaining your approachability.

DO NOT...Wear Phone Accessories During the Meeting

If you sit through an entire meeting or meal wearing an earpiece, headset or any other hands free answering device, you send a powerful nonverbal message: **you're not giving the other people in the room your full attention.**

Nonverbal communication speaks before you do. It accounts for 93% of your communication. So, along with eye contact, smiling and open body language – barriers like cell phone headsets will nonverbally send the wrong message, for example: "Please anticipate our meeting being interrupted by somebody who's more important than you."

DO NOT...Let Your Phone Ring More Than Three Times

Some cell phone rings are unbelievably loud. If this is the case, try to silence the ringer after three beeps – or in some cases, symphonies. Odds are you're annoying the heck out of someone else in the room, namely, the person sitting two feet across the table. Most cell phones have buttons on the outside that double as ring silencers. Use them. Consult your manual and learn how to quickly silence your phone while it's still in your pocket or clip.

DO...Wait for the Right Time

The best time to check missed calls you politely silenced is when you or your colleague is away from the table. This will give you enough time to see who you missed and, if need be – return an emergency call. And if you must return the call immediately, don't do it at the table. Politely say, "Please excuse me for a minute, but I have to take this call."

Some people will pretend to use the bathroom for the sole purpose of making a phone call. This *can* be an effective technique, but be careful. If you've had a few glasses of water, ten minutes later when you actually *do* have to go to the bathroom, you'll turn into "The Boy Who Cried Hello."

DO NOT...Insult the Absent

Have you ever seen people answer their phones during a meeting or meal and try to compensate for their rudeness by insulting the person on the other line? Unbelievable. Here's how the four step process goes:

1. They roll their eyes
2. They give the other person at the table the "just a minute" index finger
3. They impatiently bob their head back and forth to the rhythm of their boring conversation
4. They form their non-phone hand into the "Quack Quack" gesture which symbolizes someone else on the other line who won't shut up

Meanwhile you're sitting there like an idiot, feeling bad for the person on the other end of the phone, deciding whether or not you should have another roll.

Ouch. This is not approachable behavior.

DO NOT...Assume People Sitting Next to WON'T Hear You Divorcing Your Husband

One winter I got stuck in O'Hare Airport on a weather delay. (Big surprise) And while enjoying my heart-clogging Cinnabon roll, my ears puckered to a voice coming from the table next to me. I glanced at the lady who was talking on her cell phone so loud; the entire restaurant could hear every word of her conversation.

And to make matters worse, she was divorcing her husband.

I kid you not.

"Well I don't care how much money is in the bank! I am entitled."

"You never listened to me in the first place Ron!"

"Do you think I LIKE talking to you this way?"

This soon-to-be-single woman taught me that cell phones are amazing things – not because of their advanced technology to keep our world connected, not because of the camera capabilities, and not because of internet browsing options – but because of their roles as shields. Here's what I mean...

When people talk on phones, they tend to spill their guts without consideration of those in their immediate presence. It's as if the person on the other line is the only one who hears them, when in actuality someone sitting two seats down may or may not have just learned about an intimate, personal bit of information. The lesson to be learned is:

If a cell phone conversation has personal content, take it to a personal location.

DO NOT...Debate the Caller ID

Nothing is more frustrating than to be on the other end of the "Caller ID Debate." Not unlike the Third Person Insult you just read about, this also runs through a four step process:

1. They give you the "just a minute" index finger
2. They check their caller ID
3. They tilt their head and stare at the phone for 2-5 seconds
4. They make a decision to answer the call or return to your conversation

This is terribly uncomfortable. You actually watch your friend (?) decide whether or not there's someone else she'd rather talk to. Once again, not approachable behavior.

✦ ✦ ✦ ✦ ✦

Cell phones have become *the* primary form of communication. In fact, manufacturers shipped 585 million phones in 2004, according to a study from market watcher Strategy Analytics. But with every phone shipped comes a coefficient of frustration caused by improper etiquette.

So, show consideration for the person joining you and be mindful of ringers, accessories and incoming calls. And if you use your cell phone at the right time for the right reason, you will honor your company as an effective communicator.

Remember: don't incur the opportunity cost of cell phone convenience at the expense of people sitting right across the table. You're sitting down with THEM. Talk to THEM!

HOW TO LEVERAGE YOUR VOICEMAIL INTO AN EFFECTIVE MEDIUM OF COMMUICATION

And then...there's voicemail. The medium of communication most overlooked and underused:

"Hi this is Annie. Leave your name
and number and I'll get back to you."

This is an example of a typical outgoing message – and it makes callers feel like they really *are* talking to a machine. Now, we all hear this cookie cutter message about a dozen times daily. And it doesn't necessarily make a voicemail message bad; but it does mean the voicemail is not being *fully leveraged*.

Have you ever left a message on someone's voicemail who obviously recorded their greeting in a car?

"Hi you've reached the voicemail of (HONK!) I'm away from my (HEY WATCH WHERE YOU'RE GOIN LADY!) but I'll call you back as soon as I (SCREEEEECH!) Thank you."

Beep.

Click.

Messages like these will make your callers feel unimportant. Messages like these will show your callers you don't care enough about them to spend 10 lousy minutes recording a clear message. But not for long. Let's go over a few points for recording an AMAZING voicemail message.

The first rule of transforming your voicemail is: **get rid of the noise**.

When you go into your office or home – shut the doors, turn the music and TV off, and record your message in absolute silence. Not unlike conversation, your voicemail is a medium of communication. And like any medium – robotic or otherwise – noise is a barrier.

Once you've secured a quiet atmosphere with your phone, it's time to figure out **what you're going to say.** What's more, how you're going to say it. Think of your business cards, website, letterhead and promotional materials: what makes you stand out? Is it the slogan? The phrases? The company name?

I used to sell furniture at a family-owned store in Portland called City Liquidators.[1] Every week the owner, Pam, would re-recorded a new voicemail with one or two amazing furniture deals. She did this so her customers – even before walking into the store – knew their prices were the lowest in town.

Unfortunately when it comes to voicemail, businesspeople just seem to go through the motions. They throw some generic message together and it stands out like a needle in a stack of needles. But remember: everyone uses voicemail. Everyone. So, what are you going to record to allow your callers differentiate you from all those other "I'm away from my desk" people out there?

Let me ask you this...
Who has the best voicemail greeting you're ever heard?

Here's another question: Why can't voicemail messages be **fun**? In search of an answer I recently consulted my Sprint PCS Handbook. I found the following instructions under the section called "How to Record Your Outgoing Message":

> *When recording outgoing voicemail message, remember to sound as unfriendly, boring and bland as possible to guarantee maximum robotic presence in the minds of your callers.*[2]

Not bloody likely.

[1] www.cityliquidators.com
[2] Not actual text from handbook

I have a friend whose greeting says, "Hey this is Jeffery. Leave me your 16 digit American Express Card number and I'll get back to you soon. Thanks!" Believe it or not, at least three callers a day actually leave their credit card numbers for him! In fact, the first time I called him I gave him my card number too. Guess that explains the $2,000 bill on my statement.

But the advantage to a message like this is that it shows your true colors. And people love that. So, unless you actually *are* a robot – don't sound like one. Sound like you. People like and want you.

If you call my office[3], you'll hear a message like this:

"Hello, my name is Scott – and you have reached Front Porch Productions. Sorry I missed you; but leave me a message AND tell me your favorite thing to do on a Sunday, and I promise to call you back! Thanks, and we'll talk soon."

Every month I change the question. (This recording was from July '04) But to my surprise, my callers' responses immediately transformed according to their level of *engagement*.

Great example: Once, my answering machine asked a question about the caller's favorite place to eat pizza. During that particular month I received a call from a local business in St. Louis interested in working together. The woman left her information along with, "Oh, and I LOVE Pizza Hut. In fact, Scott," she joked, "you can go ahead and send a few pizzas over to our office. We've got 24 hungry employees down here!"

So, I did the same thing anybody would have done in my position:

I ordered four large pizzas to be delivered to her office.

Now, I placed my order BEFORE I called her back. Then I dialed her number, introduced myself and thanked her for interest in my services. I then asked if she'd like to set up an appointment. She agreed to meet the following day.

"All right, I'm looking forward to seeing you tomorrow Scott," she confirmed.

"Cool – sounds good!" I said. "Oh, and by the way – those pizzas should be arriving at your office in about 20 minutes."

"Ha ha ha...you're so funny Scott! See ya later."

She thought I was kidding.

Exactly 13 minutes later, I received an email from her:

"Scott!! I can't believe you sent us pizza!! I thought you were kidding! Everyone loves them – thanks so much. We'll see ya tomorrow!"

[3] Give me a call! (314) 878-5419

105

As you can see, people are more willing to open up to your voicemail when they are asked a fun, open ended question. What's more, once personal preferences are revealed via self disclosure – trust, rapport and common points of interest will develop in the relationship. Not to mention, it's easy to leverage someone's message as a great ice breaker when you return his or her call!

OK...now once you're ready to record your voicemail (with a script to read from), there's only one thing left to do: **smile**. I know, it sounds so simple. So cliché. So Dale Carnegie. But say the following sentence aloud: "I'll get back with you in 24 hours."

Now say the following sentence WITH A SMILE: "I'll get back with you in 24 hours!"

Did that make you feel silly? Maybe.

Did that sound totally different? Probably.

But does it matter how it makes *you* feel? No. It matters how it makes your *callers* feel. It matters if your voicemail makes callers actually feel your smile through the phone.

There are two reasons to record your outgoing message with a smile. First, it will sound like you actually took the time to record your message instead of quickly spurting out a few words while merging onto the interstate. What's more, people will believe you **do** care about their call.

Secondly, you never know who's going to call for the first time. Imagine getting a phone call from a new referral with valuable potential to generate a lot of business. She leaves a message and awaits your follow up. Now, odds are if you met her for the first time **in person**, you'd be smiling so much your ears would get crowded. Likewise, if your voicemail is the first time she hears your voice, speaking your smile is a great way to make a first impression. Even if you're not there!

Let me ask you this...

How could you make your voicemail more engaging and fun?

The bottom line is: **your voicemail is a communication tool with untapped potential.** If you take a few extra minutes to rerecord a unique, fun, engaging and friendly outgoing message consistent with you or your business's personality, here's what will happen:

YOUR CALLERS WILL...
- Smile as they leave a message
- Be able to separate your voicemail from the other 1000 they call every week
- Tell their friends about your voicemail, who will also call you
- Hang up feeling glad they called you
- Feel a connection with you because their interaction – even if it was with your voicemail – made them feel comfortable and engaged.

We depend on our technology on an hourly basis. Without our cell phones, laptops and wireless connections – we'd feel helpless. But that doesn't grant us permission *replace* face to face interaction with it. Instead, use it as a *supplement*. It's your job to send emails, answer phones and set up voicemail so the people you're communicating with **feel like you're right there sitting next to them.**

Whether you're connecting via email or phone, there's always a way to manifest the power of approachability to become an effective, engaging technological communicator.

P O W E R P R I N C I P L E # 6
BEING APPROACHABLE MEANS CAPABILITY OF BEING REACHED

CHAPTER SEVEN

It Ain't About You

Developing Mutually Valuable Relationships through Networking

"If you go out there looking for a friend, they'll be scarce.
If you go out there being a friend, you'll find them everywhere."

ZIG ZIGLAR

BEFORE WE BEGIN THIS CHAPTER, LET'S TEST YOUR EXISTING KNOWLEDGE on networking:

1) The best definition of networking is...
   a) Schmoozing at meetings and events
   b) The solicitation of funds
   c) Building and maintaining mutually valuable relationships
   d) Marketing and selling your products and services to everyone in the room so you can meet your sales quota before your boss fires you

2) Why do you network?
   a) To develop your business
   b) To help other people
   c) To share information
   d) All of the above

3) What are the most effective ways to network?
   a) Regularly attending meetings, events and activities
   b) Talking to random people in the streets, stores, busses and bathrooms
   c) Offering referrals, resources and recommendations
   d) It doesn't matter as long as you help others first and remember it's not just about you

4) True or False: Networking is not a skill, but a hereditary trait passed down from your father not unlike height or Male Pattern Baldness.

5) True or False: Networking isn't always strategic, but frequently occurs by an accident and/or stroke of luck which falls in your lap like a gift from God.

(Answers will be available at the end of this chapter)

Networking is a term that didn't exist (academically) until almost 40 years ago. It's a word uttered in and around the business world every day, yet is unclear to most as to how it actually works. Still, it's a fundamental tool to the success of any business.

In this chapter, you will learn:

- What networking IS
- What networking ISN'T
- How to leverage both strategic and serendipitous networking into mutually valuable relationships
- How to become a Networking Superhero

WHAT IS NETWORKING?

Networking is the development and maintenance of mutually valuable relationships. It's not schmoozing, it's not handing out business cards, it's not selling, it's not marketing, and it's not small talk. Some of those activities are *part* of networking, but be careful not to confuse form with function. Networking is a process that requires the right attitude, patience and organization.

Networking is one of, if not THE leading way to **increase your business.** In fact, I get almost 100% of my business from some form of networking. And with proper preparation and implementation, a networking plan will be your catalyst for dramatically changing the way you deal with, obtain and maintain your business relationships.

Networking is also **sharing information**. For example, every year I attend a National Speaker's Association Convention. They're a blast: non-stop learning, seminars, sessions, and of course, partying. But when I return home from events like these, I always make copies of my notes or loan out my three inch binder full of goodies to colleagues of mine who couldn't attend. That's networking.

I do this because our most valuable resource is each other. And the supply never ends! I once read a quotation from my favorite author, a philosopher by the name of *Anonymous*, who said, "Even though it's not *what* you know but *who* you know – remember that *who* you know teaches you *what* you know."

Furthermore, networking is a **skill.** Because this book is not a "how-to" book, but a "how-to-**BECOME**" book, you will discover effective networking is not an inherent trait. It takes time to develop. Clearly, some individuals are more extroverted, friendly and outgoing than others. And that most definitely helps. But anyone can develop his or her networking skills with some research and plenty of practice.

Networking is helping others. Some people just don't get it. They honestly believe it's all about them. *Wrong*. Networking is, as aptly stated by Zig Ziglar – getting what you want by helping others get what they want first. With that, let's continue as we re-visit **Power Principle #4** from Chapter 4:

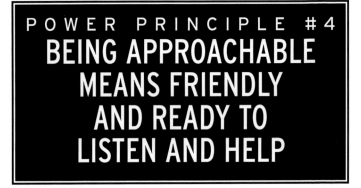

I'd like to share some ideas on the most common opportunities for networking. Because everyone has his or her preferred method, choose the ones that work best for you. Depending on your availability, financial situation and industry, some capacities are more effective than others.

Chambers of Commerce

The goal of this international organization is to help people grow their businesses through learning and sharing. It's a perfect starting point. Chambers usually have one chapter in every area. They have general membership meetings once a month and several other events throughout. I suggest you look up the websites of five chambers close to you and attend one meeting of each. After you've experienced the various styles, people and personalities of each group – pick the one (or two) that fits you the best.

What's more, Chambers are peppered with professionals from every industry. This provides you with a forum of diverse knowledge and affiliates with whom new relationships will be invaluable. And you never know what you might learn from someone who works in a different field!

Association Meetings

There's an association for EVERYTHING and EVERYONE. Look at *The Encyclopedia of Associations* to find out what national groups appeal to you. Most likely there will be a local chapter with a website and a calendar of events.

These associations are fundamental to your success as a businessperson. Not only do they keep you updated with current trends of the industry, but they keep you connected with other professionals in your field from whom you can learn a great deal. For example, I belong to the National Speakers Association and the St. Louis Publishers Association, to name a few. And I've met more friends and colleagues; shared more valuable information; and earned more new business because of the relationships I've developed through these groups over the years.

Local Groups

Even though they won't be listed nationally, there are literally tens of thousands of small groups in every nook and cranny of the country. From men's and women's clubs to mastermind groups to alumni organizations, all are excellent sources of people with whom you can share and connect. Most importantly, building front porches by discovering the CPI (Common Point of Interest) is a piece of cake!

One advantage to joining these smaller, informal groups is the limited cost. Whereas Chambers, Associations and other national organizations require nominal membership dues, getting involved with local groups is fairly inexpensive.

Professional Networking Organizations

For more experienced networkers, there are many groups that specifically require its affiliates to contribute leads, contacts, references and resources as part of their dues. These groups, such BNI (Business Network International) are excellent sources of referrals, although the cost of membership tends to be more expensive than your local Chamber.

Events and Activities

If you open the business section of your local paper, you will find a listing of local conferences, seminars, workshops, trade shows and business expos. Some are free while others charge a nominal admission fee. But all are perfect venues for learning, meeting new people and hearing some great speakers. Check this list regularly and you'll be pleasantly surprised when you find out how many different events appeal to you!

Here are a few other suggestions for groups that offer networking opportunities:

- PTA Meetings
- Neighborhood Groups
- Faith Communities
- Online Communities
- Political Clubs
- Intramural or General Interest Groups

These are just a few of the most common capacities for networking. But the best part about creating *your* networking style is this: it doesn't matter where or how or when you network, as long as **it works for your business and you remember that it's not just about you.**

Let me ask you this...

What meetings/organizations do you attend for networking opportunities?

Once at the end of a networking luncheon I attended, Susan – who I'd been talking to for a few minutes – invited me out for coffee the following week.

"Great idea," I thought, "we can share ideas and brainstorm! Let's do it Friday at four."

"Sounds good Scott!"

The following week I walked into my local coffee shop and saw Susan already seated at a booth by the window. I grabbed my coffee and plopped down next to her.

After a brief hello, Susan uttered a sentence I will never forget. A sentence that gave me chills. A sentence you never, EVER want to hear come out of another person's mouth in a one-on-one networking meeting:

"Scott, I'd like to tell you a little bit about a company called…
…AMWAY."

For those who haven't had the pleasure of being suckered into a discussion that begins with this sentence, please allow me to elaborate: *Amway is the world's most notorious pyramid scheme.* And for a measly investment of only two hundred dollars, Susan thought I might want to become involved.

I was appalled. I wanted to storm out of that coffee shop without even saying goodbye. But I didn't, because that's not the kind of person I am. So, I sat through her entire, word for word spiel. 7-10 uncomfortable minutes later, I ran out to my car faster than you could say "multi-level distribution system."

And we never spoke again.

On the way out to the car I thought ...*and I was really starting to like Susan. I figured another small business owner like me would be a good person with whom to share ideas for mutual gain.*

Guess not.

At that exact moment I asked myself an important networking question. One that isn't asked enough:

WHAT ISN'T NETWORKING?

I'd read almost every networking book out there, and never before had I see more than a few pages on this topic. Through my research, I discovered other authors and speakers who addressed the topic of networking spend the bulk of their time teaching people what TO DO – what networking IS. And I believe it's a fundamental concept to business and personal success. But not enough time is spent teaching people what NOT TO DO – what networking ISN'T. And I believe it's an equally important concept.

Susan was one of the first individuals I met who practiced the Habits of Highly Horrible Networkers™. But I knew she wasn't alone. I knew there were other people in the business world that practiced these habits. Not to mention, the victims who suffered from their habits.

So now, it's up to you and me to stop them. (Cue superhero theme music)

Highly Horrible Networkers™ think, act and react in recognizable ways. Some of these habits will shock you, especially if you've found yourself at the mercy of someone who tried to use them against you. As we move into this next section of this chapter, examine them with a careful eye. Take note of these Highly Horrible attitudes and actions so you know what to avoid while you're developing mutually valuable relationships.

THE 7 HABITS OF HIGHLY HORRIBLE NETWORKERS™

1) Attitude

Much like the development of any skill, networking begins with attitude. Unfortunately, Highly Horrible Networkers™ have the *wrong* attitude. If you've ever attended a networking function before, perhaps you've encountered businesspeople who act in the following ways:

- *The hard sell* – they believe networking is about one thing and one thing only: selling products and services to everyone in the room.
- *Business only* – they're not there to make friends. They're not there to have fun. And they're certainly not interested in developing mutually valuable relationships.
- *It's all about me* – they don't take the time to help and share with others, but rather focus on their own needs. In other words, they can't spell "N-E-T-W-O-R-K-I-N-G" without "I."

Attitude is fundamental to effective networking. In fact, it's the *most* important habit to understand. For this reason, I intentionally placed this Highly Horrible Habit *first* on this list because it has a way of underscoring all the other habits that will follow.

2) Dig Your Well WHEN You're Thirsty

One of my favorite networking books is called *Dig Your Well Before You're Thirsty*, by Harvey McKay. It's probably the most well known text on this subject. The key to McKay's work is making your friends, establishing contacts and developing relationships – before you need them. Getting what you want by helping others get what they want *first*.

Enter the Highly Horrible Networkers™, who only network because:
- They need new customers
- They have a new product or service to sell
- Their boss forced them to do so

Take my friend Lawrence, for example. He's quite successful in the insurance business; however he recently approached me about using networking to obtain some hot leads.

"My numbers are down. My boss is on my back. I gotta get out there and start networking...or else! What do you suggest?"

"Networking takes time," I explained, "and you can't expect to come into loads of business or dozens of potential clients without developing the relationships first."

As you already learned, networking is the development and maintenance of mutually valuable relationships...over time. If you try to dig your well WHEN you're thirsty, you may never find a drink.

3) Dealin' the Deck

Habit #3 is a dangerous one, and it happens all the time. Have you ever seen people distribute 247 of their business cards during the first 5 minutes of the event? They move as quickly as possible from one person to the next. They don't make eye contact, they don't ask to exchange cards – **they just deal them out.**

"Here's my card, call me if you need a designer! See ya later."

"Hi, Steve Sanders with The Bronze Buttocks Tanning Company. Nice to meet you. Here are ten of my cards. We got some great deals in December...come on down! See ya later."

This is guaranteed to make people feel puny and insignificant. Notice these Highly Horrible Networkers™ don't spend time actually *meeting* and *establishing rapport* with new people; but rather concentrate on giving out as many cards as possible. It's quantity over quality, right?

Wrong.

Dealin' the Deck is one of the most common networking pet peeves. Whenever I give my program *The Habits of Highly Horrible Networkers™*, I walk out into the audience for a quick demonstration of this habit. I grab a stack of business cards and quickly jump from table to table tossing out dozens of them without as much looking at the audience members I'm handing them to.

It's a great bit. But unfortunately during one speech, it backfired.

Literally.

I was demonstrating Highly Horrible Habit #3 at a local Chamber of Commerce meeting. While hopping from table to table as dozens of cards flew through the air and into people's laps and salads, someone yelled out, "Oh my God!"

I stopped dead in my tracks. I looked back at the head table and noticed that one of my cards landed in the centerpiece...

...which was a candle!

MY BUSINESS CARD WAS ON FIRE!!

I threw down the microphone, lunged at the table and snatched the burning business card from the candle! As I toppled over the chair in front of me I yelled something to the effect of "Holy crap!" shook the flames off my half burnt card and regained my balance to a roaring applause/laughter from the audience.

"And...uh...this just goes to show you ladies and gentleman," I fumbled, "When you deal the deck of business cards without eye contact or consideration...uh...people may as well **set them on fire** – because they're not going to read them anyway!"

Nice save.

Let me ask you this...

Have you ever returned to your office after a networking function, pulled out a stack of other people's business cards and asked yourself: "Who the hell ARE these people?"

4) Unprofessional Information

It's remarkable how often some business cards will contain unprofessional information. Have you ever received someone's card with one of those ambiguous, offensive and questionable email addresses with AOL, Hotmail or Yahoo? Not only are those email servers frustrating and ineffective for business communication, but just imagine how it looks when someone has to send business emails to:

- HotLips98@aol.com
- KaylasMommyRules@yahoo.com
- Isellcars2U@hotmail.com

I have nothing against AOL, Hotmail or Yahoo. But if possible, always send and receive emails using the address of your organization's website, i.e., scott@hellomynameisscott.com. If you **must** use free servers like MSN, SBC and the like, choose a simple username that doesn't question your professionalism, i.e., jackgateman@yahoo.com.

5) Sit with the Wrong Company

I'll never forget my first Chamber meeting. One afternoon I sat down with 6 other local businesspeople for our monthly networking lunch. Naturally, the first thing I did was look at everyone's nametags. (Not only to learn their names but to examine the effectiveness of their nametags' design and placement.)

These were the nametags I saw: Bank of America, Bank of America, Bank of America, Bank of America, Bank of America, Bank of America, *Scott*.

Highly Horrible networkers not only *attend* meetings with their friends and/or coworkers, but they **talk and sit with them the entire time**! These are people with whom they've worked 5 days a week, 8 hours a day for the past 3 years! This is not a good technique to maximize your company's visibility.

This habit creates an elitist, unfriendly attitude. And think how uncomfortable this makes the one or two people sitting at the table who *don't* work for that company! It's unfair to *them* because they're unable to meet a diverse group of people with whom to develop mutually valuable relationships!

If you're sitting with YOUR company – you're sitting with the WRONG company.

Let me ask you this...

If you walked into a singles bar with six of your friends, would you sit in the corner to talk to your friends all night?

6) Small Talk is for Suckers

Highly Horrible Networkers forget about the small talk. It's a waste of their time. They don't ask or answer about "New and exciting things happening at work" or "How Thanksgiving was," they simply jump right into (what they believe to be) the most important part of the discussion: selling 17 of their products before the salad arrives.

Has this ever happened to you? For example, has someone ever introduced themselves, breezed right through the conversation and flat out asked you for a referral?

*Refer you? I don't even **know** you!*

As you learned in Chapters 3, 4 and 5, reciprocating self-disclosure is the most effective way to build rapport and ultimately develop trust. The people you want to do business with are those with whom you *have* built that rapport and trust. So, small talk is *not* for suckers. Debra Fine, author of *The Fine Art of Small Talk* put it best when she said: "Small talk is the biggest talk we do."

7) Limitations

Finally, Highly Horrible Networkers™ believe there is only one specific time and place for networking. It's called "A Room with A Sign Posted Outside That Says So." In other words, they only network when someone forces them to. They don't believe networking opportunities in places like elevators, busses, supermarkets or parks.

Does this look familiar?

Meeting Agenda

5:30 – 6:00: Registration
6:00 – 6:30: Networking
6:30 – 7:00: Dinner
7:00 – 7:30: Speaker

That's it? A measly half hour for networking? Doesn't give you much time, does it?

The truth about networking is that it can happen anytime, anywhere.

There is a time and a place for networking – it's called ANY time, and ANY place.

Don't limit yourself to a room. Sometimes, you just never know! And in the next section, you'll learn how to treat networking with more than just a *strategic* eye. But before we move on, let's quickly review the 7 Habits of Highly Horrible Networkers™:

1) Attitude
2) Dig Your Well When You're Thirsty
3) Dealin' the Deck
4) Unprofessional Information
5) Sit with the Wrong Company
6) Small Talk is for Customers
7) Limitations

SERENDIPITY NETWORKING

As you already learned in this chapter, networking is the process of sharing knowledge, helping others and developing mutually valuable relationships. But you also learned that networking isn't always planned.

That reminds me of the Bible.

Why?

In the book of Hebrews 13:2 it says "Fear not to entertain strangers for by so doing some may have entertained angels unaware."

Please re-read the last two words in that quotation.

Angels unaware: **that's what networking is all about.**

So far we've discussed how to use networking as a strategic tool. But, there are two *kinds* of networking: **strategic** and **serendipitous.**

Serendipity is the lucky tendency to find interesting or valuable things by chance. Networking is the development and maintenance of mutually valuable relationships. Mix the two forces, and you've got a surefire formula to boost your business.

Now, I understand the Catch-22: if it's serendipity, how can you plan it? Well, you're right – you can't. But here are a few ways to be more aware of it and prepare yourself to leverage it when it crosses your path.

Have you ever said to yourself, "Boy, I sure was at the RIGHT place at the RIGHT time!"?

It's a great feeling, isn't it?

Well, here's another question. Have you ever said to yourself, "Boy, I sure was at the WRONG place and the WRONG time!"?

There's a negative connotation in that sentence, isn't there?

GOOD NEWS: There doesn't have to be...

One night I walked into Borders in search of a new book a friend recommended called *The Networking Survival Guide,* written by Diane Darling. I pulled it off the shelf and began browsing through it. After a few minutes, I noticed a large poster to my left that read:

IN STORE DISCUSSION AND READING OF DIANE DARLING'S THE NETWORKING SURVIVAL GUIDE!

TOMORROW, 10:00 AM

Oh my God! Best selling author Diane Darling – coming into *my* Borders tomorrow? Wow! What an honor!

Then I did the same thing anyone would have done in my position:

I bought the book, ran home and then stayed up half the night reading all 327 pages so I could be prepared when Diane Darling came into the store the next day.

Sure enough – bags under my eyes and all – I dragged into to Borders at 9:30 AM the next morning. I rushed to the back of the store. There in front of me was a flip chart on an easel, dozens of chairs circled around a table and of course and a well dressed woman with one of the rosiest smiles I'd ever seen.

That was her. That was *the* world renowned expert on networking: Diane Darling. Wow!

I tiptoed up to her like a typical groupie and said, "Good morning! I just wanted to introduce myself: my name is Scott Ginsberg. I bought your book yesterday and read the entire thing last night and it's such a wonderful read and I'm a big fan of your work and I wrote a few books about similar topics and...well...um...would you possibly consider signing my copy, Diane?"

She looked at me like I was CRAZY.

"Oh I'm sorry, but...*I'm not Diane Darling.*"

What the...?

"My name is Cheri Hanstein – I own a local company called Premiere Training Solutions. You see, Borders invites me into their store all the time to lead discussions about new books. Today I'll be facilitating a 30 minute **adaptation** of *The Networking Survival Guide* by Diane Darling."

Nice one Scott.

"Well, uh… it's nice to meet you…Cheri. I guess I'll have a seat," I resigned.

I later learned that the in-store posters were *printed incorrectly* and failed to mention that **Diane Darling wasn't actually coming.**

Damn it! I sure could have used those few extra hours of sleep right about now.

Nevertheless, Cheri led a great program. She discussed several points from Diane's book and encouraged the participants (all four of us) to share ideas and brainstorm effective networking techniques.

After the other audience members cleared out, Cheri began packing up her stuff. I thanked her again for her program and also apologized for my case of mistaken identity.

"Well Cheri, I guess I'll see you around…."

"You too Scott, take care!"

And the funny thing is – I DID see her around.

Everywhere.

Cheri turned out to be affiliated with several of the same organizations I was! I started seeing her at my meetings and events. Then I found out we had many mutual friends and contacts! **Serendipity** had brought us together.

And now, I'm honored to say Cheri is:

• One of my good friends
• A colleague with whom I share information, brainstorm and generate ideas on a regular basis
• One of the editors of this book!

All because I was in the **wrong place** at the **wrong time.**

As you can see, Serendipity Networking has unexpected power. World renowned speaker, author, and my friend Carol Weisman learned this same power several years ago. She was giving a speech at a conference that unfortunately conflicted with a concurrent session given by none other than management guru, Dr. Steven Covey.

Pretty stiff competition, huh?

So imagine Carol's dismay when she jumped on stage after an enthusiastic introduction only to be greeted by her **audience of FOUR people.** Ouch.

Her heart broke. Carol almost died. But, she did her absolute best and blew the audience away. At the end of her speech she announced, "And now, I'm going to do something Steven Covey would NEVER do – I'm going to take my entire audience out to lunch!"

Little did she know a member of her audience worked for PBS...Who signed Carol to a five year contract...To do a hit series...That won a TELLY AWARD!!

Serendipity is powerful. I mean, REALLY powerful. How many times have you met a valuable contact and said, "Wow! The planets must have been aligned tonight!" "The Gods have smiled down upon me!" or "What are the odds of meeting someone as perfect as her?"

Here are some warning signs that will keep you aware of serendipity as it crosses your path:

- Do you see the same person time and time again at similar meetings and events? Great! You are experiencing "Networking Dejavu," and it's not an accident. This is a person with whom you obviously share common interests. Go talk to him! There's a good chance you can help each other.
- Have you ever walked away from meeting someone at a coffee shop, bar, store, gym, church, mailbox, park, train, street corner or bus and said to yourself, "Thank God I had one of my business cards with me today!" What a great feeling! Chance encounters like these are more valuable than you think.

My favorite example happened in March of 2003 when I spoke on a panel of experts at a local trade show for Missouri Meetings and Events[1]. Copies of my first book, *HELLO, my name is Scott*, were made available to audience members in the back of the room.

Unfortunately, the audience didn't know the books were **FOR SALE.**

So, they robbed me.

129 books – out the door!

By the time I made my way back to the table, all that remained were a few of my business cards and a half empty bottle of Diet Dr. Pepper.

Ouch.

OK, it wasn't the end of the world. I'd given away thousands of books in the past four years anyway.

But still, it hurt.

Just when I thought my luck had run out, a young woman approached me. She asked if I had any other copies of my book for sale. Apparently she didn't make it to the table in time.

Luckily, I always carry a few extra copies in my briefcase. And since the audience had already stolen so many, I figured: **what the hell, what's one more book?**

As I signed the inside cover and thanked her for attending, I learned a great deal about my new friend. We discovered that our networks overlapped! Allison attended college with several people I knew. And once I learned more about the non-profit organization[2] for which she worked, we decided to stay in touch and agreed to find ways to help each others' businesses in the future.

But I never would have expected what happened next...

About a month later I received an email from a man named Paul Wesselmann[3]. Paul is motivational speaker and trainer based out of Madison, Wisconsin who stumbled upon my website. He asked if he could include a link to my website in his upcoming newsletter called The Ripples Project[4]. I gratefully accepted.

Little did I know his subscription base was 12,000 people!

Shortly thereafter, I started receiving calls and emails from several organizations and colleges interested in booking me for future programs! As a result, I had great opportunities to work with the University of Las Vegas, Nevada, the USTA (United States Tennis Association) and many more!

Paul is now a great friend of mine with whom I share ideas and stories all the time! And because of his vast experience in the speaking industry, I also consider him to be one of my mentors!

Now...can you guess HOW Paul stumbled across my website?

The girl in the audience who didn't get a book. Allison was a friend of Paul's!

That experience helped me understand how to leverage networking opportunities. It's a three step process, and here are the steps to take: Listen, Localize and Learn.

LISTEN: The most important communication tools you own are your ears. Keep them open for CPI's (Common Points of Interest) and iceberg statements (the key phrases under which 90% of the remaining important information awaits.) They are the tickets to starting and maintaining conversations.

For example, when I called Paul a few weeks later, I LISTENED to him briefly mention something about his friendship with Allison, the woman from the audience.

LOCALIZE: If you've ever been stricken with food poisoning, the first thing you always do is – OK, the *second* thing you always do – is localize your sickness. You MUST find out what food caused you to spend your

[2] www.kidsmartstl.org
[3] www.paulwesselmann.com
[4] www.theripplesproject.org

125

Friday night in the bathroom for 7 hours.

Serendipity networking is the same way. You MUST find out what conversation, interaction, event, bathroom stall writing, relationship, email, phone call, referral or website caused you to experience your moment of serendipity. In other words, discover where the rock created the ripple. In my case, I localized my new business opportunities to when I made that one friendly connection with an audience member.

LEARN: Lastly, make mental note. Make a post-it note! Do anything that will remind you of the chain of valuable events so in the future you can put yourself in a position where it is likely to happen again. Learn *why* you gained new business. Learn *why* you know who you know. Then use that knowledge to make it happen again. And again. And again.

In my case, I learned how beneficial it was to my business to say, **"What the hell, what's one more book?"**

Let me ask you this...
What have you learned from your moments of serendipity?

Still, the question remains: **Can you make serendipity happen?**
No.

But as the definition states, it means a lucky tendency to find interesting or valuable things by chance. Therefore, it IS possible to make yourself more aware of the warning signs and more accessible to that which fortuitously affects you. And even if you DO think it's all about luck, remember this: L.U.C.K is an acronym for Laboring Under Correct Knowledge.

HOW TO BECOME A NETWORKING SUPERHERO

Now that you understand Strategic and Serendipity Networking, here's an example of how to put your new knowledge into play by becoming a Networking Superhero.

Imagine you just met your ideal client at a networking event. He's friendly, shares great ideas and could use a valuable person like you to help grow his business. Not to mention, he's the kind of person from whom you could learn a great deal as well. After all, networking is the creation and maintenance of mutually valuable relationships.

After chatting away, building rapport and connecting for a few minutes – the crucial time comes: **the exchange of business cards.** At his request, you give him *your* card. Then you ask for his card in return.

And at that moment, your worst networking nightmare comes true. He utters the one sentence you never want to hear from a new and potentially valuable contact:

"I don't have one of my business cards with me right now."

Ouch.

What do you do in this situation?

Some people become frustrated with the person who commits this cardinal sin of networking. (Not a good idea.) Although business cards are the number-one networking necessity, there's no reason to make a big fuss if someone doesn't have one. Unfortunately, it happens. People may be changing jobs, reprinting or assumed they didn't need their cards at the time. But calling them out will only reinforce emotions of their un-professionalism.

A common solution to this problem is suggested in most networking books: **simply write your new contact's information on one of your own business cards**. (Not a bad idea.) But space is limited. And how many times have you written information down in your haste only to become completely baffled by your own hieroglyphics when you read your notes a week later? Also, it's possible you will later give this scribbled card to someone ELSE when you mix it in with your own stack. Perhaps this isn't your best option.

Another way to capture contact information is to use **scrap paper**. (A dangerous idea.) People do this all the time, and it's not an effective networking technique. Not only does it make you look inefficient and disorganized, but statistically: you will lose that piece of scrap paper.

Finally, there is one other way to try and solve this networking nightmare – but it usually fails.

Once after giving a speech at a sales rally, a member of the audience approached me about giving a future program for his company's national conference. I was excited to learn more about working together, but unfortunately...

...you guessed it! No business card. But he *did* say, "Why don't you just give me *your* card – **and I'll call you**..."

Reluctantly, I gave him my business card. He promised to follow up the next week so we could set up a meeting.

And do you think he ever called?

No. And of course, I was unable to call him – because I didn't have his information!

You can't depend on everyone to call *you*. It's not because they don't like you or because they're not interested in developing a mutually valuable relationship – but because people lose, forget and misplace things. They also meet lots of people every day and it's challenging to differentiate themselves among their long list of contacts.

Therefore, the question still remains: **How do you effectively and professionally capture the information of a valuable contact that doesn't have any of his business cards?**

Thus far in the field of networking, there is yet to be a solution.

Until now.

- What if there was a way to be one step ahead of every person you met?
- What if you could leverage every networking opportunity to transform new connections into mutually valuable relationships?
- And what if you could eliminate missed opportunities by helping others become capable of being reached?

There *is* an answer to your worst networking nightmare, and it's called **My Card**™. Here's how it works:

When someone reluctantly tells you she doesn't have any business cards with her, reach into your pocket and offer her **My Card**™.

"You don't have one of your business cards with you?" you empathize, "Well, don't worry about it – it happens all the time! Here you go..."

On the front of the card you hand to her, it reads in sharp blue writing: **My Card**™ – because to your new contact who doesn't have a business card, that's exactly what it is. It's her card!

"But I've really enjoyed meeting you, and I'm sure we can find ways to help each other," you explain.

"Here! Fill out the card with the best way to reach you. Then I'll hang on to this one so we can be sure to stay in touch."

And this is the best part…

"Oh – and here are a few extras for you to keep with you until you get your new cards," you say as you give her <u>several other cards.</u> **"I don't want you missing any networking opportunities!"**

No scrap paper. No scribbles. No assumptions or hopes for future contact. Just a fun, simple, memorable, face saving tool. It creates a connection between two people who want to build a relationship. What's more, when you graciously hand this card to someone you've just met, you will:

- Make an UNFORGETTABLE™ first impression
- Show her you're committed to developing a mutually valuable relationship
- Demonstrate effective networking skills
- Reinforce the idea that networking is all about them by giving them several extra cards
- Stay in touch with new people to whom you can give value

If someone doesn't have their business card, they're not capable of being reached. They're not approachable. They can't be helped, and they can't help others.

But if you pull **My Card**™ out of your pocket; tell your new friend to fill it out – and **give her a few extra cards for future use** – you will break down those barriers. You will save the *day*, save the *information* and save the *face* of the person you've just met. Not to mention, make their subsequent networking a lot easier.

You will become a Networking Superhero!

And you will turn friends into mutually valuable relationships. All because you took the initiative to empathize with someone who *wanted* to connect with you, but couldn't because they needed a front porch through which to express their inherent human desire to do so.

Interest in people's business cards means interest in <u>them</u>.

My Card™ is the answer to your worst networking nightmare – and someone else's. You'll never miss another important networking opportunity again! (Go to www.hellomynameisscott.com to order your 50 pack today!)

NAMETAG NETWORKING

The last section of this chapter will discuss an effective yet underappreciated tool to use while networking: **your nametag.** Especially when you attend meetings, events or if you're out in the field representing your company, your nametag is your best friend. Not only will it remind people of your name (who will forget it 10 seconds after they shake your hand anyway), but it will advertise your business.

If you're a small business owner or entrepreneur and you don't have your own custom nametag, you're missing out. Imagine you attend your Chamber of Commerce meeting and you get stuck wearing the obligatory, computerized, faded-font, barely-sticks-onto-my-lapel piece of junk. You will not stand out. You will not promote your business. And other affiliates will not know who you are or how you give them value. Try this: at your next meeting, sit by someone in real estate – *those* people know how to wear nametags!

Unfortunately, some nametags are **removed** at certain times during events. It's not uncommon for participants to remove their nametags when they eat, smoke, use the bathroom, go to break out sessions or attend pre/post show activities. A good rule of thumb is: don't. Leave your nametag on for the entire meeting. You never know when there will be a new person in attendance who doesn't know who you are. Remember, as my friend Jeffery Gitomer teaches, "It's not who *you know*, it's who *knows you.*"

Think of yourself as a taxi driver. If you cruised down the street looking to attract customers, you wouldn't shut off your "on duty" lights. Be available at all times to those who need your services. You never know around which corner your next customer will be standing!

During a speech for one of my clients, Coldwell Banker, I was told a story by an audience member who had great success with Nametag Networking.

"Most employees at our office wear t-shirts with our embroidered nametags on the front. Recently, I was having dinner at Applebee's while wearing that shirt. A lady stopped me and said, 'Are you a Realtor? I am in town to buy a house this weekend, could you help me?' I sold her a home two days later!"

Another key to getting the maximum mileage out of your nametag is its **consistency.** For example, all billboards for McDonald's have similar components: the golden arches, the food, the lifestyle images and the slogans. They are consistent because effective advertising campaigns coordinate their branding efforts between media. Therefore, since your nametag is just like your own billboard, make the font, color, logo and company information consistent with the existing brand of your business. As a result, when people meet you, look into your eyes and then look at your nametag, everything will synergize together as one valuable entity.

A great example of someone who uses a nametag as a branding tool is my friend Tom Terrific. Tom is an author, speaker and trainer whose company is called *Terrific Presentations*. Not only do his name, company and programming revolve around the word "Terrific," but his nametag simply reads, "Tom Terrific." And nobody ever seems to forget Tom. Why? Because he's *terrific* – and he wears the nametag to prove it!

Here's another technique used by Cal Thompson, owner of TripleXpresso's in St. Louis. He encourages Nametag Networking at his meetings with a tool called "Xpress Request." This is a way to identify networking needs in a quick, efficient manner. Here's how it works. In addition to their standard badges, people also wear pre-registered nametags with a list of three things they need, i.e., Web Design, Direct Mail, A New Assistant, and the like. This immediately lets others know how they can help!

Lastly, your nametag immediately identifies you as an **ambassador** of your company. Take my friend Bob, for example. He's a Financial Representative for Northwestern Mutual. He wears his shiny, sleek, silver nametag on the lapel of his elegant suit every day. It looks professional and meticulous. And just like his nametag, *Bob* is professional and meticulous. *Bob* is elegant.

That's an example of how to use your nametag to become an ambassador. It keeps you accountable for your behavior while you wear it. It's not unlike a logo shirt. It is the personification of your company's culture. So wear it proudly. It will help you maintain a consistency between your performance and the mission of your business.

I know, I know – nametags are silly and annoying. They ruin your clothes. They diminish your anonymity. They draw unwanted attention to certain areas of your body.

But, what if you wore a beautiful, customized nametag to *differentiate* you?

What if…your nametag offered a small amount of personal information that made you more *approachable*?

Then, the only people who *would* look silly would be those who *weren't* connecting and engaging with each other. The people who *weren't* building front porches. The people who *weren't* getting the maximum mileage out of their nametags.

Let me ask you this…

Do you have a custom nametag to wear at networking events?

Final Tips on Effective Networking

We've covered a lot of networking ground! Let's review with some final tips to help you develop and maintain mutually valuable relationships:

Get organized. At the beginning of every month, sit down and organize your networking plan. Ask yourself the following questions:

- When are the general membership meetings of my organizations?
- Whom can I meet for lunch/coffee to brainstorm and share ideas?
- What special events are coming up I want to attend?
- Are there any new groups with which I could get involved?
- Whom haven't I talked to in a while?
- What resources, tips, articles, ideas or contacts could I share with the people in my network?
- What people could I introduce who would be able to help each other?

Get out there. Networking is largely based timing. And although you can't *create* a lucky tendency to find interesting or valuable things by chance, you can still put yourself in a position to grab it when it crosses your path.

Unexpected conversations are the stuff networking is made of.

Manage Your Contacts. Whatever tool or database you use to manage your contact information – ACT, Goldmine, Outlook – find a system that works best for your goals/business. I suggest some type of database management software that allows you to update not only personal information, but the progression of communication between you and the people in your network. (A stack of business cards on your desk isn't going to cut it anymore)

And write down the names of every person you meet. And I'm not just talking about business contacts – **everybody**. You never know when, 6 months down the road, an idea will pop into your head and you'll need to call someone.

Networking isn't limited to a room. The birth of this book was a result of a conversation I had with my good friend Todd – in a swimming pool! We were taking a break from our NSA Convention when I ran a few title ideas by him. He agreed that *The Power of Approachability* was the best choice, so I decided right then and there. And as any writer will tell you: once you get the title, everything else is cream cheese.

There is a time and a place for networking: ANY time, and ANY place.

So, whatever event, meeting, conference or seminar you attend – arrive early and stay late. Sometimes the most valuable connections are made when nobody else is around. What's more, there is less pressure when you're networking on *your* time, not the *organization's* time.

Become a resource. Carry with you a list of books, websites, ideas, suggestions and articles of value for the people you're meeting with. Not only does it provide resources for them, but it gives you an easy conversation starter. Remember, helping others first DOES help you too!

Keep a pen and paper handy. *If I don't write that idea down now, I'll never remember it!* If you've ever said this sentence before, you know how valuable a simple notepad is. I recommend carrying a small pen and paper with you, wherever you go. Keep it right next to your business card holder. My little notepad is the single greatest accessory I've ever purchased in my life. It saved my butt – and other people's butts – numerous times. You can buy these at any luggage store at your local mall for under $20. Most of them have refills for the paper and a nice pen that fits inside the pad. And I can't begin to tell you how many ideas, names, phone numbers or recommended book titles I've written down the exact moment someone told me.

Stock questions. No front porch behavior is more effective than asking open ended questions. So, don't walk into a networking event without a few great stock questions relevant to the event, i.e., What's the biggest challenge of your job? What's been the most effective way to promote your business? (For dozens of other great examples, see Appendix A: "55 Great Questions to Ask Someone You Just Met.")

Stick with it. A common misconception about networking is it boosts your business right away. *Wrong.* Remember the woman from the audience who didn't get a book? She emailed a friend of hers who ultimately helped me obtain several new clients...**nine months later.** Networking takes time to reciprocate back to you. And because the process of developing mutually valuable relationships involves helping others *first*, you may not see the fruits of your labor for weeks, months, maybe even years!

Get your story straight. Have you ever heard the question, "So...what's your story?" This is an obvious figure of speech. People don't actually expect you tell them a story. But what if you did? People don't remember things, facts or ideas – they remember stories. So when it comes to business, you've got to have a story. Most businesspeople have some signature tale of how they became involved in their line of work; or something unusual that happened in their job. So be known for your story. Write it out. Tell it often. Soon, people you don't even know will approach you and ask for "your story." It's a perfect front porch.

And lastly but certainly not least...

Make your friends before you need them. In October of 2003 I joined my local Chamber of Commerce. At my first meeting I was approached by Harvey, a former Fire Chief of St. Louis. His friendliness welcomed me into the group and he introduced me to several new affiliates – a true sign of networking effectiveness.

No less than six months later, I found myself in a research rut. I was scheduled to give a speech to the Indianapolis Chapter of the Plumbing,

Heating, Cooling and Contracting Association (PHCC). The speech was approaching quickly and to my dismay, I had limited research under my belt. My knowledge of plumbing was limited to that of how to *stop up* toilets.

I desperately needed some help. At the next Chamber meeting, I asked The Chief if he knew a good plumber.

"A good plumber? Ha! I know the BEST plumber – Phil Katz. He's been a friend of mine for years. Here's his personal number..."

I scribbled down the number on a piece of scrap paper as fast as I could. This was great! The best plumber in town, and I was going to interview him for my research.

Unfortunately I sent my suit to the cleaners two days later with that piece scrap paper in the side pocket. When I picked it up, it looked like big hunk of bubble gum.

Ouch.

So much for calling Phil.

Because the speech was only a few weeks away, I started to get worried. I had no research. The next day I was driving downtown for a meeting and noticed a black and yellow van outside of my passenger window. The imprint on the door read, "Phil Katz Plumbing – Over 40 Years of Experience!"

No way.

I almost swerved into the other lane.

Unfortunately, the van exited on the next ramp, so I didn't have time to memorize the number.

Then by the power of either traffic or serendipity, **the exact same van showed up on the exact same highway three hours later.**

No way.

I DID swerve into the other lane this time!

I immediately looked at the number, and for the rest of the drive home, I turned off the radio and repeated aloud, "878-4320, 878-4320, 878-4320, 878-4320, 878-4320, 878-4320."

I called Phil right away. And thanks to The Chief, I finally got hooked up with the best plumber in St. Louis. He told me everything there was to know about becoming a plumber. And I was equipped with the knowledge to create a fantastic speech that would have otherwise been flushed down the toilet.

In the beginning of this chapter you tested your knowledge of networking by taking a short quiz. Now, let's review the same questions again, and see if any of your answers have changed.

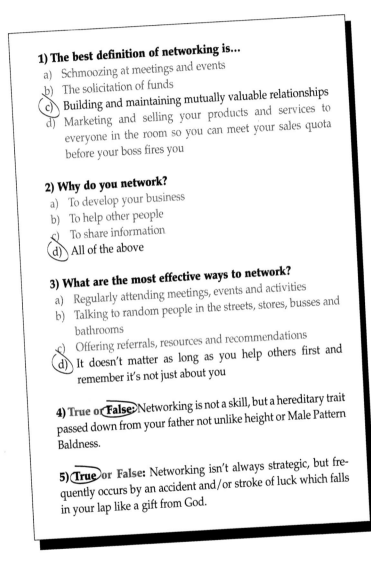

1) The best definition of networking is...
a) Schmoozing at meetings and events
b) The solicitation of funds
c) Building and maintaining mutually valuable relationships
d) Marketing and selling your products and services to everyone in the room so you can meet your sales quota before your boss fires you

2) Why do you network?
a) To develop your business
b) To help other people
c) To share information
d) All of the above

3) What are the most effective ways to network?
a) Regularly attending meetings, events and activities
b) Talking to random people in the streets, stores, busses and bathrooms
c) Offering referrals, resources and recommendations
d) It doesn't matter as long as you help others first and remember it's not just about you

4) True or False: Networking is not a skill, but a hereditary trait passed down from your father not unlike height or Male Pattern Baldness.

5) True or False: Networking isn't always strategic, but frequently occurs by an accident and/or stroke of luck which falls in your lap like a gift from God.

I hope you now have a greater understand of what networking IS; what networking ISN'T, and how to use nametags and the power of serendipity to your advantage as you develop mutually valuable relationships. Networking, however, is only one component of business success. Now let's move into Chapter 8 and learn more about how to build front porches...WITH CUSTOMERS.

CHAPTER EIGHT

Building Front Porches... WITH CUSTOMERS:

Approachability is *Avail*-ability

"There is nothing that doesn't matter. Every word is a seed that scatters. Everything matters."

GLEN PHILLIPS OF TOAD THE WET SPROCKET

As you learned in Chapter 2, **FRONT PORCHES** CREATE COMFORT, BREAK THE ice, empower communication and build rapport. But now it's time to build *business* front porches by taking those four functions and adding on the following designation: WITH CUSTOMERS. Before we continue, let's review **Power Principle #5** from Chapter 5:

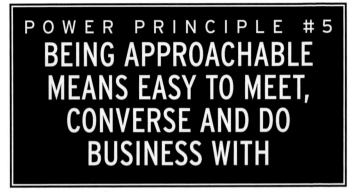

P O W E R   P R I N C I P L E   # 5
BEING APPROACHABLE MEANS EASY TO MEET, CONVERSE AND DO BUSINESS WITH

Now, it's my responsibility – as the world's foremost field expert on nametags – to start this chapter by answering some of the most frequently asked questions about employee nametags. After all, one of the most common front porches used in business today is a nametag – which keeps you on stage...WITH CUSTOMERS.

FAQ: Are first and last names necessary for employee nametags?

Anonymity and personal safety are two issues to be taken into account when providing nametags to employees. Most handbooks or employee manuals briefly mention their nametag policies, however many businesses fail to address this issue to its fullest extent. Many employees won't feel comfortable working with their first *and* last names on their nametag. I've heard accounts of nosey customers who tried to contact – even stalk – employees outside of work because they obtained their personal information from their nametags.

One solution to this problem is to print first name only nametags. This protects the anonymity of the employee, maximizes the space and looks friendlier. If a situation arises where a person's safety is in jeopardy, I suggest keeping an extra nametag with an alternate spelling, or even a different name.

FAQ: On which side of your chest should you wear a nametag?

In mid 2003, I received a letter from Wake Forest University from a man by the name of Eben Alexander, Jr. MD. He heard about my front porch philosophy on an interview I did with CNN, and wanted to send his regards. Here's the letter he sent:

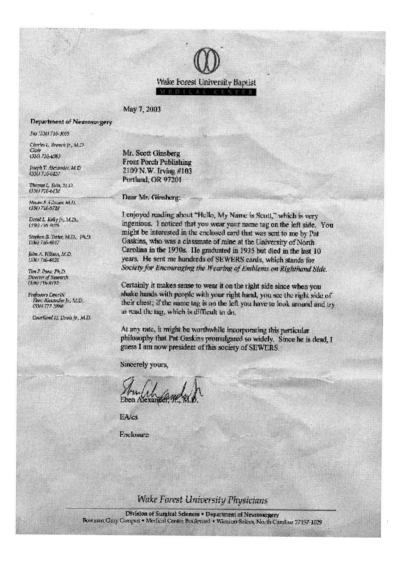

As the president of SEWERS, Dr. Alexander also offered me a lifetime membership to the organization. He sent me the following membership card:

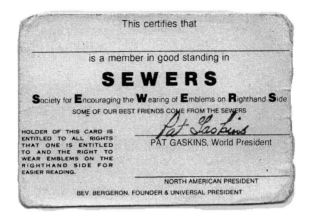

This certifies that

_____

is a member in good standing in

S E W E R S

Society for **E**ncouraging the **W**earing of **E**mblems on **R**ighthand **S**ide

SOME OF OUR BEST FRIENDS COME FROM THE SEWERS

HOLDER OF THIS CARD IS ENTITLED TO ALL RIGHTS THAT ONE IS ENTITLED TO AND THE RIGHT TO WEAR EMBLEMS ON THE RIGHTHAND SIDE FOR EASIER READING.

Pat Gaskins

PAT GASKINS, World President

_____
NORTH AMERICAN PRESIDENT

BEV. BERGERON, FOUNDER & UNIVERSAL PRESIDENT

In my first book, *HELLO, my name is Scott;* I illustrated how picky I was about wearing my nametag on the LEFT side. I've always worn it this way because I feel it's most accessible to those walking in my opposite direction on the left side of the road/hall/street. Because I encourage others to engage from a larger proximity, it certainly makes more sense.

But every book on networking, meeting planning or interpersonal communication instructs people to **wear nametags on their right side.** "They" say to wear your nametag on the right hand side so it is visible in the direct line with your handshake. For the most part, I agree. And so do most businesspeople. In fact, this is the only nametag protocol people are familiar with.

But for once, it's time to set the record straight. As the world's *only* expert on nametags, it is my duty to give you the truth – the *whole* truth.

It doesn't matter which side of your chest the nametag lays, as long as it's above your breastbone and readable from 10 feet away.

NOTE: A few weeks after I got the letter from Wake Forest, I wrote Dr. Alexander back and thanked him for his kind words, explained my differing theory on chest placement of nametags, but regretted to inform him I was unable to join SEWERS. However, because of Dr. Alexander's willingness to help – I still keep his membership card with me at all times. (For more information about nametags, please refer to **Appendix F:** The Nametag Guide)

FAQ: What are some tips for wearing nametags at trade shows?

Before you even pack your show, make sure your employees, sales-people and booth representatives each have THEIR OWN pre-made company nametags. You can get these created at any local engraving store for less than $7 a piece, probably cheaper en masse. The reason to do this is because trade show nametags rarely maximize your "nametag real estate." Also, trade show nametags rarely include your logo – which is key for brand recognition. The trick is, wear 'em both!

Next, when you get to the show, wear your own custom nametag in a visible location so everyone who walks in and out of your booth sees it. Potential buyers need to make the instant connection between YOU and the BOOTH. Also, when you get busy, it can get hard for prospects to locate the right person for assistance. The last thing you want is uncertainty about who the actual booth employee is! So use your nametag to identify and dif-ferentiate yourself among the masses.

FAQ: Are there alternatives to employee nametags?

The profession most commonly associated with nametags is food serv-ice – and rightly so. If there's anyone whose attention you must be able to grab ASAP, it's the person delivering your food!

But like so many people, I too worked in food service for many years as a waiter, busboy, bartender and food runner. So I know the value of self-disclosure through the offering of names to expedite and effectively provide excellent service.

Recently I ate at an Italian restaurant called Macaroni Grill. If you've never been to this franchise before, I highly recommend it. (Stores are located around the country.) On the other hand, if you're on a low carb diet, I suggest you avoid the establishment at all cost because the bread is AMAZING.

Anyway, the handbook has a strict policy about nametags: employees don't wear them, they *write* them. This is their alternative to employee approachability. When the server comes to the table to greet the guests, he or she takes a crayon and writes his or her name on the white paper table-cloth – upside down. (It's fascinating the first time you see it!)

So, when my server Josh scribbled his name in perfect all-caps, upside down right in front of my Diet Coke, my face lit up!

"This is great!" I thought, "I'll never forget his name."

Josh reminded me about one of the limitations of nametags worn by service agents: **they're only visible when the person is near you.** As a result – even if the server *does* wear a nametag – odds are you'll forget his name the moment he walks away. After all, a person's name *is* the single context of human memory most apt to be forgotten.

But think of all the times you went out to eat, forgot your waitress's name and desperately needed some ice water, ketchup, the bill or a booster seat – but couldn't get her attention because you forgot her name. It was frustrating, wasn't it?!

At Macaroni Grill, you won't forget your server's name. You can't. It's right in front of your face during the whole meal! This level of the server's approachability makes it easy for you to grab his attention when you need it.

On the other hand, some restaurants don't even use nametags. I learned this from one of my favorite local restaurants in St. Louis several years ago. The waitress approached the table and I noticed she wasn't wearing a nametag. This didn't upset me in the least bit; after all, nametags aren't for everybody. But in the middle of the meal I became disappointed: **she never once gave me her name.**

I got the attention of the manager as he perused the aisles.

"Hi, I'm Jeff the manager, how is everything this evening?"

"Great as usual Jeff," I replied, "but I have one question about your waitresses: do they NOT wear nametags, or, did our waitress just forget hers today?"

"Actually Scott, we don't believe in nametags. I think nametags serve a purpose for some restaurants, but not ours. Our servers are trained to introduce themselves to all their guests when they greet the table."

Oh really...

Nameless service notwithstanding, Jeff made an excellent point: it's not about nametags – it's about making the customers feel welcome. It's about approachability. And servers must do this by introducing themselves thereby making their constant service **available** to those who need it most.

✦ ✦ ✦ ✦ ✦

These answers to frequently asked questions will help you create and wear your nametags more effectively. But as you know, nametags are only *one* of many front porches you can use to become a more effective, engaging communicator one conversation at a time...WITH CUSTOMERS.

As you recall from Chapter 2, **a front porch is any object or behavior that increases approachability.** You also learned, in the chapters that followed, various ways to apply that concept with your first impressions, conversations, technology and networking. Now, let's bring several of those situations together and specifically apply them to various interactions you have with your customers.

The system we will use in this chapter is called The C-BEB™ Model, which is based on the four characteristics of front porches. It will help you epitomize approachability in your business interactions so your customers will feel comfortable, welcomed, engaged and connected to you. This model will also allow you to maximize *availability*...WITH CUSTOMERS. The components are based on the following **characteristics of front porches:**

- **C**reate Comfort...WITH CUSTOMERS
- **B**reak the Ice...WITH CUSTOMERS
- **E**mpower Communication...WITH CUSTOMERS
- **B**uild Rapport...WITH CUSTOMERS

The C-BEB™ Model
PART 1: Front Porches Create Comfort... WITH CUSTOMERS

As I mentioned in Chapter 1, Wal-Mart was the first business to require all its employees to wear nametags because Sam Walton wanted **the customers to get to know the people they bought from.**

But the value of approachability spans far beyond getting to know people. It's all about *Creating Comfort.* In other words: inviting customers to step onto your front porch. So whether you work in retail, hospitality, food service or sales, to wear a nametag is to be on stage. To be on stage is to be ready to serve your customers. And to be ready to serve your customers is to do your job effectively.

The most important rule in retail is "Make a friend in thirty seconds."

The quickest and surest way to do this is to inform and remind customers of your employees' names. This creates comfort in the conversation. And when you put your customers at ease, the sales process will be more personable.

On the other hand, customers often have difficulty finding the employee they're looking for. Imagine you walk into a store. You browse the aisles for a few minutes and decide you'd like to speak with a sales associate. You look around, see a few browsers, but nobody appears to be an employee. After wrongfully asking and embarrassing a few strangers who don't actually work there, you get frustrated and leave the store. As you walk out the door, you complain, "Darn it! Doesn't anybody work here?!"

Nametags also contribute to a **synergized workplace.** Have you ever started a new job and didn't know everyone's name until the third month? Or what about the organization for whom you've contributed ten years and still don't know the name of the curly haired girl from the second floor? Let's face it: people are terrible with names. So for organizations with hundreds of employees, nametags for your teammates will only ease their pain and contribute to a synergized, more connected workplace.

Employee nametags are also **free advertising.** A nametag is just like your company's billboard! (Except it's free and people will actually look at it for more than three seconds.) So, when customers or clients work with your employees, they will be exposed to your logo, colors and brand identity. As a result your nametag turns into an effective medium for free advertising. A well designed nametag will constantly keep your company's brand, logo and corporate culture in the minds of your customers and prospects.

Furthermore, **nametags are fun**. Kids like them. Adults like them. They promote friendliness in the workplace and foster a sense of community. And customers want to spend their money in places, on items and with people who are welcoming and approachable. Next time you walk into Borders, take a closer look at one of the employees' nametags. Often times their lanyards will have stickers or pictures of their favorite books on them. Employees who wear fun, memorable nametags will also show the customers their *business* is fun and memorable.

Nametags also keep employees **open for business.** Perfect example: I have a bad habit of putting too much hot sauce on, well...everything. Recently, after I wolfed down a Tobasco covered bite of my cheeseburger, I realized I desperately needed a refill of ice water to regain feeling in my lips. My server walked right by, but unfortunately I failed to get his attention because I didn't know his name. Why? You guessed it: he wasn't wearing a nametag! No water for me.

Fortunately I chugged down my date's ice tea.

A nametag makes it easier for customers to gain the attention of an employee from whom they need service. Without it, the customers will either find someone else to help them, or won't get what they need.

Finally, nametags transform your employees into **ambassadors.** I touched upon this in the last chapter, but let's go a bit further. If there was ever a profession that promoted the use of nametags, it's real estate. And if there was ever a person *to know* in the industry of real estate, it's Gordon Gundaker, president and founder of Coldwell Banker Gundaker Realty. In the time I've worked with CBG, I've found Gordon Gundaker to be a business person who most epitomizes being an ambassador of the company. He's one of the most approachable people I've ever met – not to mention he's been wearing a nametag for over 30 years!

"Everyone knows CBG is the best in the business," Gordon explained, "but when you throw yourself out there every day, wearing your nametag – it continuously reminds customers *who* you represent. And they know you're prepared to give them value."

Nametags immediately identify employees as ambassadors of the company, they keep them accountable for their behavior and promote good word of mouth for their business. In order to achieve the highest levels of performance success, you must begin with effective interpersonal communication. You must welcome customers onto your front porch. With properly designed and implemented nametags, you will begin to synergize your employees and *Create Comfort*...WITH CUSTOMERS.

The C-BEB™ Model
PART 2: Front Porches Break the Ice...
WITH CUSTOMERS

The opportunities to build *behavioral* business front porches between you and your customers are endless. These encounters are fundamental to the most important interaction you have with you customers: **initiation.** This brings us to the second component to the C-BEB™ Model, *Breaking the Ice*...WITH CUSTOMERS.

Let's go back to Wal-Mart for a minute. Not only were they retail nametag pioneers, they were also one of the first retail businesses to have "Greeters" at their doors. Greeters have become more popular over the years as customer "loyalty" has moved to the forefront over customer "satisfaction." Stores now want customers to come back, not just be satisfied. Businesses are now ensuring that all customers/patrons feel welcome and at home.

Enter the Greeters. They offer directions, information and most importantly, a warm welcome as soon as customers walk in the door. When I retire, it sounds like the job for me! (This is the epitome of approachability!)

I once noticed a Greeter at a local restaurant called O'Charley's. I was a bit thrown off because I didn't think *restaurants* had Greeters other than the hosts.

I walked through the doorway as I rolled my sleeves up to enjoy a typical Midwest 65 degree November day. The Greeter noticed me roll up my sleeves and joked, "Welcome to O'Charley's. And Scott, I don't want you starting any fights in here!"

I laughed as I toured the lobby area. "Well, you never know," I laughed, "I may just have to crack some heads around here..."

This Greeter, whom I later learned was known as "Bubbles," had a great story to tell. Bubbles was a frequent patron at this location years ago. Every week she and her bridge club ate there. Eventually, the managers began to take notice of this lady who was so friendly to all of the O'Charley's staff. After a while, they offered her the position on a part time basis to become their Greeter.

Bubbles has now worked there for over two years and still remains the *only* Greeter at any of the nine Missouri O'Charley's locations! And I guarantee; *that* location is the friendliest of them all!

Bubbles throws herself out there all day, every day – but it's for the customers. And that's what being **available** is all about.

Here's another example of using front porches to *Break the Ice...*WITH CUSOMTERS. Last year my grandmother Mimi was going the process of moving out of her condo and into a senior community. Although this was a necessary and exciting change in our family's life, it was slightly stressful.

Part of this process was putting the condo back on the market. With limited real estate knowledge, our family was not sure how it would pan out, or how long it would take. However, one afternoon my Grandmother – and her agent – entered the building and saw a strange lady curiously walking around the lobby. They approached her, said hello and Mimi asked, "I'm not sure we've met before...do you need any help or information about this building? I've been living here for almost 20 years!" (*Note the effective execution of asking an open ended question to encourage engagement.)*

"Well, my husband and I are in the market for a new condo," the stranger replied, "I heard about this place and wanted to check it out to see if it would work for Jim and me."

"Oh, would you like to see my place? I just put it on the market! In fact, this is my agent right here!"

"Well I couldn't do that, I..."

"Aw come on, it's right this way!" Mimi said.

Sure enough, Mimi took the lady into her apartment while her agent showed her all of the amenities and rooms.

"Wow! This place is amazing! I am so impressed, it's beautiful! It's perfect! Please don't sell it to anyone. Don't let anyone else come in here. I have to call my husband Jim. I WANT THIS CONDO!

And that was that. The bidding process began, the contracts were drawn up and the deal was closed several weeks later. A new resident moved into her dream home, and my grandmother made a smooth transition into the next phase of her life. All because she broke the ice, threw herself out there and stepped onto someone's front porch – that just so happened to be a potential customer!

Let me ask you this...

How do you break the ice with your customers?

The C-BEB™ Model
PART 3: Front Porches Empower Communication...WITH CUSTOMERS

You've already learned the value of *Creating Comfort* and *Breaking the Ice*. But when you build front porches between you and the customer, you also create an opportunity to learn about them. What's more, you create an opportunity to learn about your business. Therein lays the value of the third element of the C-BEB™ Model, *Empowering Communication*...WITH **CUSTOMERS**. Every conversation, interaction and encounter possesses the power to teach you something.

Keep even the smallest details in mind. Size, contrary to popular belief, doesn't matter. There is value in every mundane interaction *and* every customer you serve. You never know what you might learn!

Do you recall how to "Turn Water into Lemonade" from Chapter 3? This was one of the essential elements from the UNFORGETTABLE™ System. It involved giving Flavored Answers to Fruitless Questions to encourage others open up, stop and engage with you.

A few years ago while working at the Ritz Carlton, I discovered how to use this behavior as an effective business front porch. I saw a guest slump out of the taxi at 11:30 PM. He grabbed his garment bag and trudged to the front door.

"Good evening – welcome in! How are you tonight?" I greeted.

"Eh...fine, how are you?" he mumbled.

"Tired," I replied.

He stopped in his tracks.

"I'm sorry, did you say...*tired*?" he inquired.

"Yes sir. It's been a long day, we've been extremely busy and I'm ready to finish up my shift and go to bed!"

His body language shifted. He smiled. He set his bag down by the door...

"Yeah, I'm exhausted myself," he explained with a hand running through his messed hair. "First, my flight was delayed a few hours. Then I laid over in Atlanta, missed my connection and just arrived in St. Louis *now*. And I have a big meeting tomorrow and all I want to do is go to sleep. By the way – I've never stayed here before. Where's the front desk? Is there still room service? And do you think I can get a wake up call at 5:30 AM."

"Absolutely sir! I'd be happy to show you inside. The front desk is right this way. And don't worry," I grinned, "room service is available 24-7 at this hotel."

"Thanks a lot Scott – it's such a relief to finally be here."

OK...let's go back to the beginning of that story for a minute. What did he say the first time I asked "How are you?"

Fine.

He was "fine." In other words, "Feelings I'm Not Expressing."

But when **I opened up myself to him first**, he was empowered to share his feelings and ultimately allow me to serve him better.

Let me ask you this...

How do you empower your customers to open up to you?

The C-BEB™ Model
PART 4: Front Porches Build
Rapport...WITH CUSTOMERS

The final component of the C-BEB™ Model is *Building Rapport*...WITH CUSTOMERS. When I worked in guest services at Ritz Carlton, my job was to do exactly that: build rapport with guests. However, out of all the thousands of ladies and gentleman I served, only one guest comes to mind when I ponder the tremendous value of building business front porches: Nick.

I was struggling through work at the Ritz on a biting January Monday. The night wasn't going well: I was dropping keys, stalling stick shifts and slipping on the ice. All in all, I was in a terrible mood.

Then a red Chevy skidded into the drive. I reached for the door as the passenger tried to open it, but he couldn't unlock it. The door froze shut! After jostling the door for a minute, he finally plopped out with a frustrated grin on face.

"These darn rent-a-cars, every one of 'em is a piece of junk!"

"Yeah, I can relate sir – we park hundreds of them a day. May I offer to get you a nice Mercedes from our parking garage?" I joked.

"Ha!" he chuckled, "how about you make it a Bentley and we'll call it even?"

"Absolutely Sir, it's my pleasure! And enjoy your stay at the Ritz Carlton St. Louis."

BAM!! 100 dollars.

Wow! I'd never gotten a 100 dollar tip before. What a generous guest!

"Hey thanks a lot Mr. Innerbichler!" I said as I scoped out his luggage tag.

"Nick. Just call me Nick."

After bragging to all of my coworkers for the next half hour, I settled down to look at my hundred dollar bill: it was real. "Today is truly a great day," I thought.

But not as great as Tuesday.

On Tuesday Nick arrived at about 4:00 PM in a cab on his way back from a meeting. I, of course, ran like a Beatlemaniac over to his car so I could be the first to extend my welcome.

"Good afternoon Nick, welcome back! How was business today?"

"Long, but good. Nice to see ya again Scott. Here ya go..."

BAM!! 20 dollars.

"Hey thanks a lot, I really appreciate your generosity!"

"By the way Scott, how's my Bentley coming along?" he inquired.

"Oh I'm workin' on it Nick...don't worry. I promise I'll get you that Bentley..."

A few hours later I had an idea. Considering the generous tips from those first encounters with Nick, I felt it was time to take my service to the next level. I wanted to give back to him; thank him for being such a generous guest of my hotel. And because I made a promise to Nick, I wanted to be a man of my word.

So the next day I did the same thing anyone would have done in my position:

I went out and bought Nick a Bentley.

I had never actually *seen* a Bentley before, but I knew there was a dealership about 15 minutes from my house. I drove out there before my shift. I walked into the spotless showroom amidst some of the classiest, fanciest and most expensive cars known to man.

"Hey there *Scott*," the salesman grinned as he looked at my nametag, "Can I help you with anything today?"

"Yeah...um...I'm here to buy a Bentley."

"Oh-kayyy..." he quirked, "Which model were you thinking about?"

"Well, do you guys sell any of those miniature ones?"

"Oh...you mean the *toy model* Bentleys? Of course! They're in our gift shop over here."

Fifty dollars later, I was the proud owner of a new Bentley. What a deal!

I got into work at 2:00 PM on Wednesday afternoon. Anxiously awaiting Nick's arrival, I examined every single car that came in the drive. No sign of him. Meanwhile, his Bentley warmed up in the valet booth.

According to our schedule of arrivals, Nick was due back at around 6:00 PM. So I spent the next 4 hours imagining the following scenarios in my head:

- Nick will gratefully accept the Bentley and give me a thousand dollar tip.

- This incident will somehow get back to my boss, who will promote me.
- Nick will be so amazed at my willingness to go completely out of my way and take care of him; he will hire me to take over his multi-billion dollar engineering company.
- Because of the unpredictable St. Louis weather, Nick will be forced to cut his trip short and I will be the proud owner of a $50 paper-weight.

And then he pulled into the drive.

Same frozen red car, same black suit. He slid out of his seat and started walking very quickly towards the door, and he didn't look like he was in a good mood. Darn it. Reverting back to my days as a benchwarmer for varsity football, I took the angle of pursuit and cut him off right at the welcome mat on the front drive.

"Hey Nick, welcome back. How'd everything go today?"

"Eh...ok."

"Well, I just want to tell you how grateful I am for your generosity. We truly value gentlemen like you at this hotel. And since you've been so nice to me this week with your gifts, today – I brought *you* a gift."

"You what?"

"That's right sir – I brought *you* a gift!"

I raced back into the booth, snatched the bag and almost fell flat on my face as I returned to Nick two seconds later. I took out the box and handed it to him.

"What the...?" he wondered as he opened the box, "Hey look at this! A Bentley! Just what I've always wanted! Hey, you're all right with me Scott! Thanks a lot man!"

"Well Nick, you took care of me, and now I'm taking care of you. That's why they call it guest service. Besides...

...I TOLD you I'd get ya that Bentley!"

If you want to go the extra mile for a customer, start by taking that first step onto his front porch.

Any object or behavior that increases approachability: *that's* a front porch.

And that's just the beginning. Whether you use nametags, humor or flavored answers to fruitless questions – do whatever you can to build the instant connection between you and the people you serve.

As we end this chapter, remember The C-BEB™ Model for Building Business Front Porches...WITH CUSTOMERS:

C – **C**reating Comfort
B – **B**reaking the Ice
E – **E**mpowering Communication
B – **B**uilding Rapport

When you put the C-BEB™ Model into practice, you will walk into work every day with the tools to create comfort, break the ice, empower communication and build rapport...WITH CUSTOMERS. No matter what you do, what you sell or whom you work for, remember this: you've got to throw yourself out there! You must *approach,* and *become approachable to* customers to keep them coming back forever!

CHAPTER NINE

Hey...Who's the New Guy?

How to Solidify Awesome Hospitality for Your Affiliates, Volunteers and Guests

*"Let me live in a house by the side
of the road, and be a friend to man."*

SAM WALTER FOSS

SO FAR YOU'VE LEARNED HOW TO BUILD FRONT PORCHES IN NUMEROUS AREAS OF your life. In the first part of this book, you discovered how to build front porches in your daily interactions, your UNFORGETTABLE™ first impressions and your conversations by making yourself ready to engage, accessible and open. Then, by adapting those concepts to the business world, you learned how to become easy to connect and deal with via your technologies, your network and business life.

Now our focus will evolve into a bigger, more communal realm: building *organizational* front porches.

An *organization* is any group of people organized for a particular purpose, such as:

- Associations
- Clubs
- Faith Communities
- Professional Organizations
- Small Groups
- Neighborhoods
- Non-Profits

The effectiveness of any organization's front porch is a function of its hospitality – that of its affiliates, its staff and the group itself. In this chapter we'll take a closer look at approachability as it pertains to the connectedness of groups, namely, The New Guys. Those are the individuals who benefit the most from your willingness to extend yourself. And if you recall from Chapter 3, the willingness to extend yourself was the third **Power Principle** of approachability:

POWER PRINCIPLE #3
BEING APPROACHABLE MEANS BEING AVAILABLE TO OTHERS

When I began wearing a nametag all day, every day, the type of individuals with whom I most frequently interacted was strangers. (They still are.) And I love it! It's a an beautiful thing when throwing yourself out there can combat the coarsening of our fear-laden culture.

But when I started my *business* a few years ago, I joined several organizations, clubs and groups and began to feel the reciprocity of hospitality. As The New Guy – not to mention the young guy – existing affiliates welcomed me with open arms. They gave me the inside track on the organization. Some even offered to take me under their wings! And I was grateful. I was comfortable. What's more, I felt *welcomed*.

Biblically, the term "hospitality" relates to *philoxenia* – the Latin term for "the love of strangers." And "stranger" is defined as "someone with whom you have not yet been acquainted."

Therefore your objective as a builder of organizational front porches is: **extend love to those with whom you have not yet been acquainted.**

Hospitality is broken down into two parts: **attitudes** and **actions**. In this first section, we'll explore four Awesome Attitudes to get you into the right state of mind for building organizational front porches.

ATTITUDE OF AWESOME HOSPITALITY #1: Beyond Hello

Hospitality is more than just saying hello. Nobody understands this element of hospitality better than my friend DeWitt, a veteran hotel doorman. The first time I met DeWitt was on a crisp fall morning on the front drive at the Ritz. I introduced myself and he gave me a solid handshake, a cheeky smile and pat on the back. He started telling me all about hospitality and gave me some great tips to make the guests feel welcome.

After a few hours of check-ins and getting to know each other, DeWitt said something I'll never forget:

"Scott, I want to sell you a boat."

"You...want to sell me...a *boat?* Oh-kayyy...what *kind* of boat...?"

"Well, it's not really a *boat*. It's more of a ship: Friend*ship*, Fellow*ship* and Relation*ship*. What do you say?"

I'll take it!

That is the essence of Awesome Hospitality. Not just saying hello. Not just introducing yourself, but offering a new person your friendship, fellowship and relationship.

ATTITUDE OF AWESOME HOSPITALITY #2: The Golden Rule

Hospitality is also an expression of the Golden Rule, which as you know is "treat others as you want to be treated." Everyone knows this phrase. It's been ingrained into our minds and souls by our parents, our teachers and our mentors.

But does everyone *practice* the Golden Rule?

Here's another way to look at it: Do you remember when YOU were The New Guy? Did people extend themselves? Did you feel welcomed? If so, you probably connected with new people immediately, took an active role in the organization and felt proud to be a part of it. If not, you probably never came back to another meeting again.

I remember when I was The New Guy. I walked into my first National Speaker's Association meeting amongst some of the strongest, smartest and most well known speakers in the city. And there I was – some young guy who had only been in the business a month. I was terrified.

But several of the affiliates epitomized approachability when they offered such hospitable gestures as:

- "If you ever have any questions, give me a call!"
- "I'd be happy to watch you speak and offer my feedback."
- "Let me introduce you to some other veteran affiliates, they'd love to meet you."

What's more, now that I've been involved for a few years, I try to reciprocate that same hospitality to new speakers *I* meet. I've had a great opportunity to have coffee and share my experiences with several people who were once in my position. Because I want them to feel how I felt: **welcomed.**

ATTITUDE OF AWESOME HOSPITALITY #3: The Member Mindset

It's impossible to talk about any organization without using the word **member.** Think of the groups of which you are a member – what does that mean to you?

You might say "Being a member allows me to be part of the group," or "Being a member means I get to go to all the meetings." But most people see membership as *entitlement*:

Members are entitled to...

Here's what you get with your membership...

These are the benefits to being a member...

I looked up *member* in several dictionaries and none of them said anything about entitlement. I didn't see anything about paying dues to get exclusive benefits. The dictionary simply defined "member" as *one who belongs to a group or an organization.*

When did this Member Mindset evolve into "What stuff do I get when I join?" People forget being part of an organization relates more to *serving* others, and less to do with *being served by* others. It's like the old saying goes, "The more you put it – the more you get out."

My local Publisher's Association is a great example. As a board member, I walk into every meeting with one question in mind: How can I serve the other affiliates? What can I do to share what I've learned?

I'm known for bringing copies of articles, references, new books or even sharing a story or two with the group about successes/failures I've experienced as a lesson to those new (and old) to the business. That's what being a "member" or *affiliate* is all about.

ATTITUDE OF AWESOME HOSPITALITY #4: Everyone is a Greeter

If there's any group of individuals who extend their organizational front porch by serving new people, it's the Greeters. Talk about throwing yourself out there! During one of my programs at a Hospitality Conference, I asked my audience of 300 people to stand up if their position was "Greeter."

About 25 people got up.

I thanked those who stood and asked the remainder of the audience to give them a hearty applause.

When the clapping died down I said, "Without Greeters like these, building front porches in any organization is tough."

I then said, "But what if a new affiliate – let's call him Terry – came to your group. He walked in the door, looked around for a minute and felt a bit lost. Then Janet, an existing member, noticed Terry's behavior and decided to approach him. She struck up a conversation and they connected immediately! And all the while, Janet made Terry feel welcomed, comfortable and part of the group.

A few minutes later, let's say Terry asked, 'So, Janet...are you one of the Greeters here?'

And Janet said, 'No – I just wanted to welcome you to our group.'"

I just wanted to welcome you to our group.

I then repeated my original request to the audience:

"Now, let me ask you this one more time: please stand up if you are a Greeter for your organization."

300 people got up out of their chairs. It was beautiful. And I reminded them that **everyone is a greeter.** That is the essence to the *Attitude of Awesome Hospitality.*

Let me ask you this...

Would you consider yourself one of the greeters of your organization?

Now, before we move on to some specific ways to transform **attitude** into **action**, let me tell you about the strangest phone call I ever received:

One evening in April of 2003 I came home to the following message on my answering machine:

> *"Scotty my boy, my name is Dr. Joseph L. Pollack, calling all the way from Philadelphia. You don't know who I am, but I'm 81 years old, a retired professor of philosophy and a huge fan of yours! Don't worry, I'm not a crazy old man or anything – I used to work for President Nixon's Office years ago. Well anyway Scotty, I'm so proud of you. You're such a fine young man. I've heard all about your book and I wanted to tell you how much I support your ideas! Hey I tell ya what kid: you ever come to Philly – you got a place to stay! And if you had time, I would be honored to talk with you. So give me a call, here's my number..."*

Convinced one of my friends was playing a joke on me, I listened to the message a few more times. Finally, I decided this strange old man *was* sincere and I called him back. Minutes later, when I told him who I was, he burst with excitement! He couldn't believe I actually called him! And for the next hour, he told me stories about his position as a high school teacher and administrator in Philadelphia. Also, Dr. Pollack also offered himself as my personal tour guide if I ever made it out to the city. Talk about brotherly love!

Unexpectedly, a few months later I planned a trip to Philadelphia to see my friend Samantha. So, a few weeks prior, I called Dr. Pollack and told him the good news.

"Oh that's great Scotty! We're gonna have so much fun! I can't wait to show you around my city. Come over Friday morning at 10:00!"

So, on the second day of my trip, I set out to meet this intriguing man. I followed his directions downtown and finally arrived at the foot of a 26 floor high rise. When I made my way to his door, I knocked only to hear a faint, grumbling mutter: *"Who's there?"*

"Hello…uh…this is Scott Ginsberg – we talked on the phone about getting together today. I'm that guy with the nametag."

Dead silence.

I knocked again, this time a bit louder.

"Dr. Pollack – it's me, Scott! We were supposed to get together at 10:00…?"

About 30 seconds later, the locks began to rattle. The door opened. And standing in front of me was an 81 year old man, hunched over his cane who gazed at me through a pair of Harry Carey glasses like I was crazy.

Oh God, please tell me this is the right apartment.

Then, the man looked down at my nametag, looked at my face, burst into laughter and said, "SCOTTY!! HEY HOW ARE YA KID? GREAT TO SEE YOU, COME ON INSIDE!!"

He gave me a huge hug! I walked into his apartment and noticed piles of unopened mail, magazines and peanut shells. The air smelled like a combination of old textbooks – and feet.

He sat me down and started telling me more stories about teaching high school, asked me questions about my recently published book, and showed me pictures of some of his old friends, namely, Richard Nixon.

I continued to listen in sheer amazement of this fascinating, dynamic man. Then he offered to take me on a tour of the city! We rode the elevator down to the lobby, hopped in a cab and drove around Philadelphia – from the First Continental Congress to the famous Reading Market. We even enjoyed some authentic Philly Cheesesteaks together.

Finally we wrapped up the day and returned to his apartment. As we rested, we chatted some more about family, relationships and life. I felt like Mitch in *Tuesdays with Morrie*. And at 4 PM, I regretfully told him I had to return to my friend Samantha's apartment. As I put my jacket on, Dr. Pollack thanked me again for spending the day with him and gave an eloquent soliloquy I'll never forget:

"I've taught thousands of students in life. I love to talk to and connect with everybody. But more than anything, I love making friends and developing relationships with interesting people around the world – because those people are my most valuable resource. That's how I validate my existence. So, in every relationship you have, it's more than just being friendly – you must open your heart and your home to new people every day. You don't do it because someone tells you to; you do it because it's the right thing to do. And nobody ever needs a reason to do the right thing."

That is the *Attitude of Awesome Hospitality.*
That is the epitome of approachability.

✦ ✦ ✦ ✦ ✦

Now it's time to make the transition from **attitude** to **action** and learn some of the most common behaviors to empower you to extend hospitality to those who need it most. Remember, approachability is a two way street: you must approach, and be approachable *to* others. Starting with The New Guys.

You've probably noticed several references in this chapter to "The New Guys." These are individuals we all know. (Including us – because we've all been there before!) Now, they're not actually "Guys," as in *men.* New Guys can be anyone. And regardless of age, gender, race or personality, **spotting** The New Guys and stepping onto their front porch is your duty as an existing affiliate of any organization.

Most New Guys adhere to a standard of New Guy Protocol. Let's start with **eye contact.** Eye contact is the number one indicator that conversation is desirable. In other words, when people avoid eye contact, what they're actually avoiding is an interaction. When you see The New Guys walk in to the room; stop dead in their tracks and a) stare blankly into space, b) check out every person who walks by and/or c) meticulously examine every crack in the beautiful white ceiling – it means they need you.

As I explained in Chapter 2, one of the major engagement motivators is *to learn.* If you notice The New Guys' wandering eyes, figure out what you could help them learn. Perhaps they're looking for someone specific, maybe they've never been inside the building before, or maybe they're just checking out the crowd to see what kind of group it is. But their eyes are wandering because they're looking for answers – from someone like you.

Involvement Shields

Closely related to lack of eye contact is a psychological barrier many New Guys put up called an *involvement shield*. (We touched on this briefly in Chapter 5 in reference to cell phones.) It's exactly what it sounds like: **an object to keeps them involved and shields communication.**

A perfect example of an involvement shield is an official printed program. Whether it's a church bulletin, speaker outline, announcement sheet or just the schedule of events, isn't it amazing how long some guests will spend with their noses buried in something so mundane? Do you honestly think The New Guys are SO immersed in that engaging, one page schedule of upcoming events, they've actually been re-reading it over and over for the past 10 minutes?

Or is it possible they're staring blankly at the piece of paper thinking to themselves: Ok ... *the meeting should start pretty soon so if I just sit here and look like I'm completely involved with this stupid agenda nobody will come up and bother me and then I can eat my salad and get the heck out of here before anyone realizes I'm The New Guy.*

Other common involvement shields are:

- Cell phones
- Promotional tables with information and free giveaways
- Snack/buffet table
- Signage on the wall
- Centerpieces

Sitting Alone

New Guys don't often arrive with other people. And because they're usually on their own, it's not uncommon for them to sit by themselves. Here's a great tip: every meeting you attend, take a few minutes to look over the room. Find out who's sitting alone. Take note of the seats on either side of the person to see if they're taken. If it appears there's room for one more, politely ask to join them.

Most likely they'll be thrilled you stepped onto their front porch and inform you about their association with the group. This is a great opportunity to inform your tablemates about all the ins and outs of the organization. Give them the scoop – in a non-gossipy way – about the group and all the other affiliates you know. This will help them determine who they'd like to meet in the future. Also offer yourself as an available contact for just about anything. Try saying, "Hey – I've been a member for a while now, so if you need anything or have any questions, I'm here for you." There's no better feeling than the security of having *at least one friend* in a new organization.

Inconsistency

Inconsistent clothing is another telltale sign someone is new to the organization. If you belong to a group that maintains a casual and comfortable dress code and someone you've never seen before walks in with a three piece suit, you can bet he's one of the The New Guys.

Or the speaker. This reminds me of a speech I once gave at a church. I remember walking into the building on that warm September morning only to be greeted and surrounded by hundreds of churchgoers in their shorts, football shirts, jeans and tennis shoes. As for me, I wore my brand new, snazzy blue pin-stripe suit just back from the tailor.

Looked like *I* was The New Guy!

But I wasn't alone. The usher showed me to my seat in the front of room, right next to the stage. I grabbed my bulletin. It explained that following my portion of the service, a man named Greg Stefano was scheduled to give a short speech about his local business.

Then I noticed the person sitting next to me was a clean cut, mid 40's man dressed in a stunning three piece suit.

"You must be Greg Stefano!" I asked.

"And you must be Scott – the nametag guy!"

Indeed.

Timing

One of the toughest parts about being The New Guy is confusion about when to show up. Even when people look at the meeting time on the website, in the brochure or on the bulletin, unless they've been there in the past, they won't have the insider information on when most of the regulars arrive.

If you get to the meeting and see someone who's obviously been there for at least 15 minutes prior to your arrival, they're probably new. Also, if during the program, a meeting, service or speech you observe someone sneak in the back of the room unnoticed by most of the audience – they're also probably new.

Hey, it's tough being The New Guy. It's uncomfortable; you don't know anyone and you stand out like a sore thumb. But we've all been there before. Past experiences should motivate us to take it upon ourselves to become greeters – even if we're not designated as such – and extend hospitality to those who need it most.

These techniques for "Spotting the New Guys" are excellent ways to build front porches for your organization. But now let's take a look at some other specific behaviors you can use as *Actions of Awesome Hospitality*.

ACTION OF AWESOME HOSPITALITY #1: Go Beyond the Door

My friend, Pastor Bob Farr of the St. Peters Church of the Shepherd, told me about a woman he encountered after the worship service one Sunday. Bob went into the lobby to say goodbye to some of his friends. He noticed a woman standing alone by the coffee kiosk, so he approached her. He introduced himself and thanked her for coming.

In a reserved tone the guest said, "You know Pastor, I've been coming to this church for the past 9 weeks. I know I'm shy and all, but **not one**

time did anyone say hello to me."

"Really?" Bob asked, "You know, our staff works very hard to be hospitable and friendly to everyone – especially new people. I'm surprised nobody approached you!"

"Well," she continued, "I am usually greeted at the door when I walk in, but that's it. Once I get through the lobby and into the service, I feel invisible. Anyway, this morning I told myself: today is the 10th and final time. It's my last chance. And if nobody says anything, I'm outta here. But, thanks to your hospitality *beyond the door*, I think I'll stick around."

Have you ever felt this way – like someone made the initial effort to extend hospitality but his or her willingness trickled away after a few minutes? It's kind of like ordering your food at a restaurant, getting the food *delivered* by your server, and you never saw her again until the check came! (As if delivering the food was all that mattered.)

Shep Hyken[1], motivational speaker and author of *The Loyal Customer* and *Moments of Magic*, explains "Someone's assessment of excellent service is measured in proportion to the amount of time you spend after what's basic, needed or expected." So not unlike "Going Beyond Hello" in the *Attitude of Awesome Hospitality*, the first step in the *Actions of Awesome Hospitality* is also Going Beyond...the door, that is.

Let me ask you this...

Do you continue to welcome new people after the first 20 minutes?

ACTION OF AWESOME HOSPITALITY #2: Talk to Strangers

One of the reasons we have difficulty going beyond the door and extending ourselves to The New Guys is because we're afraid of talking to strangers. We live in a culture of fear which tells us strangers are different, and therefore, will hurt us. (Ironic, isn't it – hospitality means "the love of strangers.")

This fear finds a way of manifesting itself into our actions. Take public speaking, for example. It's the number one most common social phobia of humans. Why? Because we're afraid of being negatively judged by others – and our performance is a reflection of that fear.

But do you know what the second most common social phobia among humans is? According to the Social Anxiety Association, it's *talking to strangers*. Lyn Lofland, in her book *A World of Strangers*,[2] explained it perfectly: "Active avoidance of contact is constantly boosted by the fear of contamination from those who are not like us."

Wow. Contamination. What a powerful word. Combine that with our inherent fear of rejection – albeit by a person we don't even know – and it's no wonder people don't feel welcome at so many organizations!

But as the definition states, a stranger is someone with whom you have not yet become acquainted. Some people make strangers out to be a lot scarier than they truly are. And in the process of becoming an effective and engaging communicator one conversation at a time, you must have the courage to transform a stranger into a neighbor and neighbor into a friend. That's what hospitality is all about.

Let me ask you this...
When you attend meetings, do you talk with your friends or with the new people?

ACTION OF AWESOME HOSPITALITY #3: Dismiss Judgment

A few days before giving one of my *Awesome Hospitality into Authentic Relationships* programs, I had dinner with my best friend (and mentor) William Jenkins. I asked him what he thought the major challenges to organizations were, to which he replied with this story:

"Every year when I used to teach high school English, about a week before classes began the administration sent us our student lists. Some teachers – the *moment* they got their lists – marched right back upstairs and spent the next hour making roll changes. They selected specific students they didn't want (or who didn't seem to belong) in their classes and switched them out.

"I took that time to get a cup of coffee!" In fact, I didn't even look at my class list until the day classes began – **because I was going to teach everybody the same.**"

² *A World of Strangers*, Lyn Lofland, Basic Books, 1973

Anytime someone new walks into the door, the room or the organization, dismiss your judgment about him or her. Even if guests look like they won't fit in – they still deserve your hospitality.

I've had my share of experiences with this issue. Since I started my business, it's been tough as the only twenty-something affiliate in organizations, groups and associations in which all of the members were 10 or more years my senior. I've certainly felt my share of "shunning" by those unwilling to accept me in spite of my youth.

But over time I became more involved – even held leadership positions in those groups. And after a while some of the veterans dismissed their judgment about me and extended themselves. We discovered we shared a great deal in common – a lot more than they (and I) thought!

ACTION OF AWESOME HOSPITALITY #4: Sacrifice Your Comfort

As I explained earlier, the reason humans are so terrified of public speaking is because of the fear of being judged. But in addition to *talking* in front of scores of new faces, simply *being* in front of scores of new faces can be uncomfortable. And at every meeting of every organization, there's a good chance The New Guys will experience this fear when they walk into their first meeting.

Let's take your professional association, for example. Imagine your monthly meeting takes place on a cold, winter morning at your local banquet hall. All the board members, staff and veterans show up a few minutes ahead of time at about 7:45 A.M. (They gotta get the closest seats and the hottest food!)

At 8:06, when the program begins and most affiliates have already sat down to eat, in walks Aly, a newly registered member. She's already in a bad mood because she had to park seven blocks away. Huffing into a room full of strangers, hair out of place from the walk, she scopes out a place to sit. She feels terrible for showing up late and tries to be as inconspicuous as possible. To her dismay, only one seat remains: **the seat all the way in the front of the room.**

Aly reluctantly makes her way up to the front, turning beet red as the group watches her every move. Finally, after whispering an apology to the speaker, she sits down and takes out her notebook.

Has that ever happened to you before?

It's happened to me on a number of occasions. And not just because I have a non-existent sense of direction and couldn't arrive on time if my life depended on it, but also because veteran affiliates are often unwilling to sacrifice their comfort for someone new.

Here's another example that once happened in one of my own meetings. At the end of the evening, the president asked, "Are there any new members in the audience tonight we haven't recognized?"

A woman in the back said, "Well, some guy named Jim walked in the room at the beginning of the meeting, but he couldn't find an empty seat – so he left."

A silence fell over the group.

I looked over to the chair next to me, where nobody was sitting. It was the only empty one in the house. Well, almost empty: someone had put their jacket and scarf over the arm.

Ouch.

If you've been a member of an organization for six months, a year or five years – you've already become accustomed to the group. You're all settled in. **And you've had enough time to get comfortable.** Now you must reinstate the Golden Rule for the sake of The New Guys and *temporarily sacrifice* your comfort. Extend Awesome Hospitality to the one person who so desperately needs to feel welcome. If you don't, they may never come back again.

Let me ask you this...

Are you willing to sacrifice your comfort for someone new?

And don't assume other people – greeters or otherwise – will do this. If everyone assumes someone else will take action, nobody will take action. That's called **diffusion of involvement.**

Here some other *Awesome Actions* you can use to ensure the comfort of any new affiliate:

- Give up your seat in the back
- Park as far away as possible
- Bring someone new into your conversation

- But a raffle ticket for someone else
- Ask someone new to join your table
- Invite a newcomer out with your group after the meeting
- Allow the new person to talk as much as possible

ACTION OF AWESOME HOSPITALITY #5: Success Sentences™

Essential to the success of your organizational front porch is learning not only *what to* say, but *what not* to say to guests. This last *Awesome Action* examines several sentences, phrases and questions to avoid so you can maximize the comfort of conversation.

For example, if you walk up to someone and the first words out of your mouth are, "Do you remember me?" I guarantee you will a) make him feel uncomfortable, b) pressure him into giving an answer, and c) cause him to lose face when he regretfully tells you he can't seem to remember who you are.

Some people are good with names; others are good with faces; while others can't seem to recall a single person they've ever met in their lives. But no matter what type of memory a person has, "forgetting someone" is one of the most embarrassing feelings anyone can experience – especially if he or she has met you several times before.

I once ran into a woman I'd only met once – and it was an **entire year** before I saw her again. While I could remember *who* she was, I was having trouble with her name.

Fortunately, after we talked for a brief minute I was relieved when she said, "Well Scott – it was great running into you...and again," she said as she pointed to herself, "the name's Carolyn Black – hope to see you again soon!"

If you know someone doesn't remember you, rescue him. Just tell him who you are.

SUCCESS SENTENCE™
"Hi! I'm Scott with Front Porch Productions – we met last month at the Chamber Meeting when Pamela introduced us."

Now, the only feeling worse than forgetting someone is *devaluing* someone. In your organization, club or association – there are bound to be dozens, even hundreds of affiliates you've never met. That's OK. People come in and out of organizations all the time, and not everyone comes to every meeting.

But don't assume someone is The New Guy simply because *you don't know him.* Even if you think "Oh, I know everybody," there are always individuals on the fringes. Perhaps they joined the organization five years ago. Maybe they've been out of town for a few months or their schedule conflicts with certain meetings or events. So, watch your usage of the phrase **"Are you new here?"** Instead, try this:

SUCCESS SENTENCE™
"I don't believe we've met before – my name is Scott."

Next, in the situations when you're already acquainted with someone, it's still wise watch your tongue. For example, asking someone "How's work going?" is an assumption. And if you utter this phrase, it may necessitate a shoehorn the size of Shaquille O'Neal to get your foot out of your mouth.

According to CNN.com, the US rate of unemployment in November of 2004 was somewhere between five and six percent. Unfortunately, those were just the reported cases. So **don't overlook the possibility that the person you're talking to is unemployed**; was recently fired or is in the process of finding a new job.

A great example of an *Awesome Action* is to ask less specific, open ended questions to empower an engaging response:

SUCCESS SENTENCE™
"What are you working on this week?"

Lastly, in organizations where the exchange of business cards is a common practice, remember this rule: **don't give a business card to anyone who doesn't ask for it.** It's presumptuous. Sadly, the exchange of business cards is a ritual our culture de-formalized over the past 20 years. On the other hand, some high-context cultures like the Japanese view this as a sacred business ritual.

For conversational effectiveness, don't assume somebody wants your card. Think about it: how many times has someone given you one of their cards – without asking – and you thought to yourself, "OK...and *what* do you want me to do with this?"

SUCCESS SENTENCE™
Would you like to exchange business cards?

Some people don't think before they speak, and the price to pay is at the expense of their partner's conversational comfort. But if you try these Success Sentences™, you will be certain your *Actions of Awesome Hospitality* will make the other person you're engaging with feel welcome and valued.

Using Themes to Connect Shy Guests at Events

By now you've seen several examples of *Awesome Attitudes and Actions* that instill a sense of hospitality in organizations. As we approach the end of this chapter, I'd like to leave you with one final technique for building front porches between you, your fellow affiliates and new guests: **theme parties.**

"Hey Scott, would you like to go to a Bad Sweater Party this weekend?"

"A *what* party?!" I said.

"A Bad Sweater Party. Wait a minute...you mean to tell me you've never been to a Bad Sweater Party before?" asked Amber.

"Guess not," I admitted.

A Bad Sweater Party is exactly what you think it is: *A party at which the guests wear bad sweaters.* Nobody is certain where this idea originated. It's possible it came about during the 80's when ALL sweaters were bad. Nevertheless, my first Bad Sweater Party experience was, without a doubt, one of the most enjoyable events I ever attended.

And here's the interesting part: I only knew one person at the party!

One week before the party, I began to plan out my wardrobe. Looking through my drawers, I couldn't find anything that could have been classified as a "bad sweater." Phew! That was reassuring. I guess my wardrobe was *somewhat* stylish. Anyway, I figured since the bulk of the bad sweaters in the world were worn between 1971 and 1994, a thrift store was my best bet for scoring some particularly heinous gear.

When I went to my local thrift store I approached the counter and asked, "Hi, I'm looking for the ugliest, most out-dated, eye sore of a sweater known to man – got anything like that?"

"You must be going to a bad sweater party, huh?"

"Hey! How did you know?"

"I've been to a few myself. They're loads of a fun. Come on, let's see what piece of junk we can find for you today sir."

After a good 20 minutes of searching, I found my sweater. It was so bad, it was beautiful! It could only have been described as "Something your colorblind grandfather wore at a holiday Christmas Party in 1972 that, if it were any tighter, might have also doubled as a leotard."

I'll take it!

Later that night, Amber and I arrived at the Bad Sweater Party. She sported a purple, blue and turquoise gem that could have easily been stolen from the wardrobe room of the Cosby Show. And although I was slightly self conscious about the skin-tightness of my snowflake laden top – as well as not knowing anybody there – everything changed when we walked in the door...

"Hey!! What's up guys, come on in!" said the host, "Man, those are the ugliest sweaters I've ever seen! I love 'em!"

"Thanks man! Your sweater sucks too! My name is Scott – I'm a friend of Amber's."

"Well it's great to meet you, thanks for dressing up! Anybody with a sweater as ugly as that is welcome in my house! I'm Joe, come on in."

When I walked in, I saw sweaters of every decade, every color, every style and every brand. It almost became a game to see who was wearing the worst sweater of all. The best part was – everyone's clothes were *horrible,* and nobody seemed to care! The crowd roared with laughter and beamed with positive energy. Everyone talked to everyone. Everyone complimented everyone. And for the next four hours, I experienced the most unbelievable sense of hospitality, comfort and approachability with a group of complete strangers.

When I got home later that night, I realized that themes – especially outrageous ones – have several positive effects on the success of any group meeting.

Invite Only

How many times have you been invited to a meeting that didn't *sound* inviting?

"Our Chamber is having our monthly meeting Tuesday – you should come."
Great, see ya there.

On the other hand, when you hear about a theme party, it entices you.

"Come over to the South Side Chamber this Tuesday for our annual Mardi Gras Fundraiser!"

Now *that* sounds like fun!

Preparation Solidifies Commitment

Themes also encourage attendees to go the extra mile. The night of the Bad Sweater Party, I remember asking other partiers where they had gotten their bad sweaters. Some told me they shopped at local vintage stores; others said they raided their parents' closets while some even bought them on Ebay! It appeared I wasn't the only who committed to attending the event.

What Should I Wear?

Themes enhance events because they reduce uncertainty. Think about the big question you ask before attending a party or meeting: "What's the dress code?" This always creates ambiguity and often times, improper dress – over or under – will cause guests to feel uncomfortable and therefore unwilling to communicate. But with a theme, you know *exactly* what to wear, i.e., a bad sweater.

Breaking the Ice

Think of all the groups you attended where guests just sat around and stared at the wall. Exciting, wasn't it? The most effective way to break the ice at a party is to discuss your connection to the host – this discovers the CPI (Common Point of Interest). But **with a theme to your meeting, the CPI is already discovered before you walk in the door.**

It's impossible *not* to socialize with everyone. You can break the ice with anybody, anytime!

Next time you have a meeting or event, think of a way to incorporate a theme. Your guests will significantly increase their comfort level, approachability and friendliness. They will feel glad they stepped on the front porch of an organization that extended *Awesome Hospitality*.

As we come to the end of this chapter, let's review the Attitudes and Actions of Awesome Hospitality for Building Organizational Front Porches:

The Four Awesome Attitudes
- Go Beyond Hello
- The Golden Rule
- Avoid the Member Mindset
- Everyone's a Greeter

The Five Awesome Actions
- Go Beyond the Door
- Talk to Strangers
- Dismiss Judgment
- Sacrifice Your Comfort
- Success Sentences™

CHAPTER TEN

You Can't Win the Lottery if You Don't Buy a Ticket

The Three Pillars of Front Porches

*"Speak kind to a stranger, because you never know —
it just might be an angel come knockin' at your door."*

BEN HARPER

DECEMBER OF 2002. PORTLAND, OREGON. IT WAS RAINING AS USUAL. I CAUGHT the #15 bus and headed home from the furniture store – just like I did every night. I awaited my stop at Northwest 21st and Irving.

But this night was different.

This night was the most important night of my life.

This night would become the reason you are reading this book, right now.

I sat down in an open seat next to a clean cut man in his mid thirties. Once I brushed off the rain and got my shoulder bag and poncho situated, I thought to myself, "What would be a good way to start a conversation with this man? How could I step onto his front porch?"

I got it – Thanksgiving. Everyone loves talking about Thanksgiving!

I turned to him, smiled and asked, "So…what was the best part about your Thanksgiving?"

He smiled back.

"Well, I went back to San Francisco to see my family and take some time off work. And I got to relax – *that* was the best part," he nodded. "So what about you…*Scott*," he chuckled as he looked at my nametag, "what was the best part about *your* Thanksgiving?"

"I was out of town too; I'm from St. Louis, originally. It was great to see my family and spend some time with old friends. But I think the best part was eating an entire pumpkin pie by myself!"

"It sounds like you had an all right holiday to me. So…what kind of work do you do Scott?"

"Well, right now I'm selling furniture – but I'm getting into the business of building front porches."

"Building front porches, huh? You mean like, *construction*?

Kind of…

I went on to tell him the original nametag story, the front porch concept and the exciting news about my upcoming book release. The bus and the rain rolled on as he shared one of his favorite nametag stories from when he was in law school.

After a few minutes, the bus slowed down at 14th street.

"Well, this is my stop. It's been great talking with you Scott; and good luck on the book release. By the way, my name's Garrett. Here's my card. I'll buy ya a beer when your book comes out!"

"Sounds good man – I'm always looking to meet new people. Here's one of my cards too."

He stepped out into the rain and walked down the platform. I gave him a friendly salute goodbye.

And I never saw him again.

He never called. He never wrote. Probably doesn't even know I exist! (Sniff)

BUT...one week later, I got a call on my cell phone. A call that changed everything.

I was at work at the furniture store at about 9:00 AM when I looked at the display on my phone only to see a caller ID I didn't recognize.

Who the heck is calling me at 9:00 AM on a Monday morning?

Curiously, I answered the phone the same way I always do when I have no idea who's calling: *"HELLO, my name is Scott...?"*

"Hi – is this Scott Ginsberg, the guy who wears the nametag?" asked a sexy, articulate female voice.

"Um...it is..."

"Great! Well, I just wanted to tell you how excited I am about your whole front porch concept. I went to your website and I'm looking forward to your upcoming book release in a few weeks!"

"Hey thanks! I appreciate the positive feedback. But, if you don't mind me asking...

Who are you?

How did you get my cell phone number?

How old are you?"

"Oh I'm sorry, let me introduce myself. My name is Jill and I'm calling from the Portland Tribune. The reason I wanted to get in touch with you because I'd love to do a feature story about your nametag idea and upcoming book, *HELLO, my name is Scott*. Would you be interested in setting up an interview?"

My heart stopped.

"Are you kidding? Of course I would! Let's do it on Thursday!"

A few days later we met at Powell's Books in downtown Portland. And for the next hour or so, Jill and I walked around in the rain as she asked all about my experiences with wearing a nametag, the new book and my quest to help people build front porches.

And two weeks later, the **4 page article** ran on in the Lifestyle section in the December 29th issue of the Portland Tribune.

And that was, as Malcom Gladwell would say, The Tipping Point.

First, emails and phone calls started pouring in from around the world! Radio and television stations from every city in the country contacted me for interviews, articles and guest appearances. Major media outlets like CNN Live, CBS, The Associated Press, Headline News, Paul Harvey and USA Today featured my book and website on their programs and news releases!

Then, businesses, groups and organizations started contacting me about sharing my experiences and philosophies about nametags, approachability and interpersonal communication. In March of 2003, I gave my first speech – and I knew that was it. That was what I needed to be doing.

Next, I moved back to St. Louis. I started my company, Front Porch Productions. I became involved with the National Speaker's Association and developed various systems to transform my expertise, experience and research into a unique program of speaking, writing and learning tools to help individuals and organizations build front porches.

Now, at the age of 25, I am the author and publisher of two books and dozens of articles, an entrepreneur, one of the youngest professionals on the speaking circuit and "the world's foremost field expert on nametags" whose work has been embraced by people and organizations worldwide!

And here's the kicker. Everything that's happened in the past two years – including YOU reading this book RIGHT NOW – is all because of one thing:

Because one rainy December evening, I decided to sit down on a bus next to a complete stranger…and step onto his front porch. A stranger who just so happened to be…

The boyfriend of the reporter for the Portland Tribune.

Some people enter into our lives and change them forever – but only **after** we're willing to throw ourselves out there.

Throughout this book, you learned about my front porch – it's a nametag. You also learned what a front porch is – any object or behavior that increases approachability. Then, you learned how to build front porches in your first impressions, conversations, technologies, networking, businesses and organizations – so you could become an effective, engaging communicator one conversation at a time.

Now, it's time to find out **why**.

This is why you must build front porches.

THE THREE PILLARS OF FRONT PORCHES
PILLAR #1: You Will Meet New and Valuable People

If there's one valuable resource our society will never be depleted of, it's new people. There's always an opportunity to meet new people. Around every corner. In every restaurant. At every office. Everywhere.

And they're incredibly valuable, too. Even if you have no idea *how* they're valuable – just wait.

> ## Every person with whom you engage could potentially be that <u>one person</u> who changes everything.

I remember after I hung up the phone with the Tribune reporter, I called my Dad.

I was crying. Because I knew something was about to happen.

"Dad – you're not going to believe it."

"What?"

"Remember when were talking about my book a few weeks ago, and you told me I just needed to meet 'that one guy' who would change everything?"

"Yeah…"

"Well, I just met him. And he changed everything."

I believe that person is waiting for you. But you won't meet that person until you're **Ready to Engage (Power Principle #1)**. You won't meet that person until you're **Accessible and Easy to Deal With (Power Principle #2)**. And you won't meet that person until that first step onto someone's front porch is taken.

I've used this quotation before in this book, but I'll say it again because it bears repeating:

> *"Fear not to entertain strangers for by so doing some*
> *have entertained angels unaware."*
> — *Heb. 13:2*

That is the power of approachability – because you never know whom you're going to meet.

PILLAR #2: You Will Learn from Every Connection

Throughout this book you learned how to build front porches with OEQ's (Open Ended Questions), CPI's (Common Points of Interest) and Flavored Answers to Fruitless Questions. These techniques allowed you to go from HOW are you to WHO are you. And every conversation and encounter educated you because of your willingness to become **Available to Others (Power Principle #3)** and **Friendly and Willing to Help (Power Principle #4)**.

You also discovered that networking – the creation and maintenance of mutually valuable relationships – is a function of learning. Think back to Harvey, the Fire Chief from my Chamber of Commerce. He was one of the first affiliates who made me feel welcomed to the group. And because he was **Capable of Being Reached (Power Principle #6)**, I was able to obtain the contact information for a valuable resource without whom a future speech could have been given effectively.

Emerson once said, "Every man is my superior in some way – and in that, I shall learn of him." Absolutely! Everyone excels in some area in which you lack. Everyone knows something you don't. What's more, everyone knows some*one* you don't.

Think about it: did I have any idea who the guy on the bus was? No. All I knew was he was a *person,* and therefore could teach me something valuable. And he did.

PILLAR #3: You Will Be Enriched by the Reciprocation

Do you recall Nick, the guest at the Ritz Carlton? He was **Easy to Meet, Converse and Do Business With (Power Principle #5)** – as well as generous. Talk about approachable! So, I bought him a Bentley. And do you think he'll ever walk into another hotel the same way?

Or Dr. Joseph Pollack, the 81 year old man who *literally* threw himself out there, welcomed me into his home and taught me that *Awesome Hospitality* reached beyond hello. Do you think *I'll* ever walk into another meeting or an organization the same way?

Reciprocation means "to move back and forth alternately." But there's more. It's mathematical. It's exponential. And I believe every conversation, interaction; encounter, phone call, email and simple hello will reciprocate and therefore enrich your life in some way.

How, when or where it will enrich your life – I have no idea. You may never even realize it's happened. That's the nature of reciprocation. But, ask anyone who's ever experienced it before – and they'll all tell you the same thing: **but it *did* happen.**

Think about the last time you turned on the news and cursed the name of those lucky saps who won 50 million dollars the lottery. *Damn them!* Millions of dollars, and they did absolutely nothing, right?

Well...not exactly. They all did ONE thing: **they bought a ticket.**

And that's what approachability is all about. You gotta throw yourself out there. You gotta take that first step. You gotta buy a ticket.

When you walk into a room full of new faces, unsure of what to say or how to make that connection – you gotta buy a ticket.

When your customers are in need, anxiously awaiting your availability – you gotta buy a ticket.

And when you, as an affiliate of an organization spot someone new in need of a friend – you gotta buy a ticket.

Because you can't win if you don't play.

On that fateful November night when my on-campus seminar ended, I could have ripped off that little nametag **like everyone else did.** But I didn't. I kept it on my shirt. I decided to throw myself out there. I decided to buy a ticket.

And I won.

And on that rainy December evening in Portland when I stepped on the #15 bus, **I could have sat anywhere**. There were plenty of open seats. But I chose the seat next to Garrett. I decided to step onto his front porch. I decided to buy a ticket.

And I won.

I *knew* it was a crazy idea...but I *didn't* know it would change everything.

And you know what?

It was worth it.

GINSBERG'S GLOSSARY

Here are some of the new terms you learned in *The Power of Approachability* that will help you become an effective, engaging communicator – one conversation at a time. All of these terms have been used in this book, and **only** in this book. So, enjoy incorporating them into your lexicon as you build front porches in your conversations, first impressions, technologies, businesses and organizations!

Bad Sweater Party: a fun party in which everyone is required to wear ugly, out of date and un-cool sweaters for the purposes of making guests feel welcome and comfortable.

B.B.D.: also know as the "Bigger Better Deal," this Habit of Highly Horrible Networkers™ makes conversation partners feel puny, insignificant and unimportant.

C-BEB™ Model: a process of building front porches with customers that involves Creating Comfort, Building Rapport, Empowering Communication and Breaking the Ice.

C.P.I.: Common Point of Interest, which is used to create comfortable connections between new people.

Dealin' the Deck: carelessly and inconsiderately distributing dozens of business cards without the intent to actually help someone with their business.

F.I.N.E.: a monosyllabic conversation killer given in response to closed ended questions such as "How are you?" or "How's it going?" Actual translation of the term means "Feelings I'm Not Expressing."

Flavored Answer: an original, fun, honest and open word or phrase given in response to a mundane question that makes an UNFORGETTABLE™ first impression.

Front Porch: any object or behavior that increases approachability.

Fruitless Questions: ritual, mundane, closed ended questions that don't allow an opportunity to share emotions, preferences or opinions for engaging conversation.

Green Teeth Theory: a polite way to inform your conversation partner of visual, etiquette faux pas to reduce the possibility of embarrassment.

Member Mindset: the belief that being a "member" means entitlement to exclusive benefits and special gifts; rather than simply belonging to an organization in which you serve other affiliates and the community.

Networking Dejavu: seeing the same person time and time again at similar meetings and events with whom you obviously share common interests.

Networking One Night Stands: getting what you need or want from someone without thanking them, helping them get what *they* need or even calling them shortly thereafter to follow up.

Networking Superhero: a way to save the face AND the information of a new business contact with whom you want to develop a mutually valuable relationship.

New Guy Protocol: first time attendees to meetings, events and organizations who give away their inexperience by such behaviors as wandering eyes, involvement shields, sitting alone, inconsistent appearance and showing up early/later.

Orphan Nametag: second rate nametags given to late arrivals that look nothing like the nametags worn by 99% of the participants.

Serendipity Networking: a non-strategic form of networking that occurs by an accident and/or stroke of luck which falls in your lap like a gift from God.

Third Person Introduction Trick: the use of a third party introduction to help learn forgotten personal information about someone else.

Third Person Story Trick: using your own name in the third person during a story or an anecdote about yourself to help others remember your name without them suffering a loss of face.

APPENDIX A

Let Me Ask Ya This ... 55 Great Questions to Ask Someone You Just Met

Imagine you just met someone new. The formalities of names, jobs, etc. have been exchanged and you seem to be getting along famously. But before you know it, a few minutes pass – and it looks like you're running out of clichés!

Now what?

There comes a time in every conversation with someone you've just met when you must cross the chasm between "how are you?" and *"who are you?"* And, since you only have a few minutes to decide whether or not the conversation will continue, asking the right questions is the only way to make progress.

By asking engaging questions you will:

- Build rapport
- Spark creativity
- Invite people to share their experiences and preferences
- Show an interest in people's opinions and insights

The following list of "55 Great Questions to Ask Someone You Just Met" will change the entire dynamic of your conversations. The list is broken down into four sections. In **Getting to Know You,** you will find questions about personality traits, behaviors, likes and dislikes. Then in **What's Your Favorite,** your questions will uncover superlatives of people's preferences. Next, when you read **Back in the Day,** you will find questions to spark unique dialogues of past experiences and memories. Finally, in **If You Could...,** your questions will challenge the creativity and stretch the minds of the people in your conversations.

These questions are applicable in various situations. Whether you're in a business, social, family, public or academic capacity, use them any time! As a result, you will become more approachable so you can connect and communicate with anybody.

GETTING TO KNOW YOU

Do you go by a nickname?

Who is the most famous person you've ever met?

What's the one sound that drives you crazy?

What book had the biggest impact on you?

What's your preferred method of getting the news?

When driving, do you listen to CD's, tapes, the radio or nothing?

Are you a window person or an aisle person?

Are you a dog person or a cat person?

Do you prefer Coke or Pepsi?

Do you watch Letterman, Conan or Jay?

How do you relieve stress?

Who would you consider to be your hero?

Where do you most often find yourself singing?

WHAT'S YOUR FAVORITE

What's your favorite thing to do on a rainy day?

What's your favorite holiday?

What's your favorite smell?

What's your favorite cereal?

What's you favorite restaurant?

What's your favorite part of your job?

What's your favorite childhood TV show?

What is your favorite daily ritual?

What is your favorite quotation?

What's your favorite food to cook?

What's your favorite movie to watch over and over again?

BACK IN THE DAY

What was the first job you ever had?

What color was your refrigerator growing up?

When you were a kid, what did you want to be when you grew up?

When was the last time you played hooky from school or work?

What was the best prank you ever pulled off?

What was the last CD you bought?

What was the last movie you saw?

What was the best prank someone pulled on you?

What was the last concert you attended?

Who was your worst roommate?
What was the best concert you ever attended?
What is the best book you've read about your field?
What was the highlight of your (insert holiday here)?

IF YOU COULD...

- If you could pick any actor to be the president, whom would you choose?

- If you could add a single option to your car, what would you add?

- If you could only subscribe to one magazine for the rest of your life, which one would it be?

- If you could have dinner with any three people, whom would you choose?

- If you could write a book about anything, what would it be?

- If you could get back any article of clothing you once wore, what would it be?

- If you could hire any actor to portray you in a movie, who would you chose?

- If you could play any instrument, which would you play?

- If you could memorize any book cover to cover, which one would it be?

- If you could hear anyone in history give a speech, whom would you hear?

- If you could possess any superpower, what would it be?

- If you could own your own retail store, what would you sell?

- If you could live in one city for the rest of your life, where would you live?

- If you had an unlimited shopping spree at one store, which store would it be?

- If you could be any cartoon character, who would you be?

- If you could make any fictional character come to life, which would it be?

- If you could start your own restaurant, what would it be?

- If you could own one article of clothing from any movie, which would it be?

By asking any of these open ended, engaging questions, you will build instant rapport with your conversation partners. You will spark their creativity, invite them to share their experiences and as a result, show a genuine interest.

Time flies when you're engaged in interesting conversation! So all you have to do is ask the right kinds of questions, and you will cross the chasm between "How are you?" and *"Who* are you?"

52 Ways to Build Front Porches

If you check out this list on **www.hellomynameisscott.com**, click each number for a link to a special article, story, website or resource for each of the various front porches!

1) Smile
2) Make eye contact
3) Comment about someone's jewelry
4) Inquire about someone's shirt
5) Carry around an accordion wherever you go
6) Give Flavored Answers to Fruitless Questions™
7) Spice up your nametag
8) Make your voicemail come alive
9) Wear an interesting accessory
10) Pay for someone's item ahead of them in line
11) Invite someone onto your front porch
12) Wear thought provoking shirts
13) Greet everybody
14) Identify and amplify Names
15) Invite people to talk to you
16) Use other people's nametags
17) Ask people where they're from originally
18) Hug people
19) Wave someone's car into your lane
20) Harness the power of serendipity
21) Wear a nametag
22) Offer someone a piece of trivia
23) Make your email smile
24) Locate the C.P.I
25) Ask O.E.Q's
26) Tell people how you *really* feel

27) Ask the right questions
28) Notice The New Guy
29) Get to know your neighbors
30) Maximize the marketing mileage of your nametag
31) Call people the *right* name
32) Go beyond the mundane
33) Remember it's all about them
34) Talk in elevators
35) Help new people connect with each other
36) Honor the person across the table
37) Use alternate forms of nametagging
38) Change the name on your nametag
39) Remind your customers who you are
40) Share your identity with others
41) Watch out for the B.B.D
42) Throw a theme party
43) Voice your needs
44) Create a custom nametag
45) Start conversations with new people
46) Avoid the Habits of Highly Horrible Networkers™
47) Make an UNFORGETTABLE™ first impression
48) Break down communication barriers
49) Remind people of your name before they forget it
50) Initiate gatherings in your neighborhood
51) Don't Deal the Deck
52) Make yourself open for business

APPENDIX C

Not So Useless Trivia You Can Use in Conversations

- Each year on July 4th, Americans consume 150 million hotdogs, which, if you lined up end to end, would go to the moon and back 7 TIMES.

- No word in the English language rhymes with mouth, orange, silver and purple.

- Ancient clans that wanted to get rid of unwanted members without killing them would burn their houses down – hence the phrase "to get fired."

- "I am" is the shortest complete sentence in the English language.

- The most common first name in the world in Mohammed.

- The most common last name in the world is Chang.

- 672 is the the international telephone dialing code for Antarctica.

- Glue on Israeli postage stamps is certified Kosher.

- Mel Blanc – the voice of Bugs Bunny – was allergic to carrots.

- Dr. Seuss pronounced "Seuss" such that it rhymed with "rejoice."

- Sherlock Holmes never actually said, "Elementary, my dear Watson.

- Captain Kirk never actually said, "Beam me up, Scotty."

- A "jiffy" is an actual unit of time for 1/100th of a second

- The average person falls asleep in five minutes

- Money isn't made out of paper, it's made out of cotton

- Every time you lick a stamp, you're consuming 1/10 of a calorie

- The phrase "rule of thumb" is derived from an old English law which stated you couldn't beat your wife with anything wider than your thumb.

- The United Kingdom eats more cans of baked beans than the rest of the world combined.

- In 1954, Bob Hawke was immortalized by the Guinness Book of Records for sculling 2.5 pints of beer in 12 seconds. Bob later became the Prime Minister of Australia.

- In the 1977, Dusty Baker of the Dodgers hit his 30th home run. As Baker crossed the plate, Glen Burke raised his hand. Baker responded by raising his. The two hands slapped together, thus the first high-five in history.

- Each year, approximately 250,000 American husbands are physically attacked and beaten by their wives.

- The name Wendy was made up for the book Peter Pan.

- The chances of making two holes-in-one in a round of golf are one in 67 million.

- More than 2,500 left handed people a year are killed from using products made for right handed people.

- If the population of China walked past you in single file, the line would never end because of the rate of reproduction.

- In an average lifetime a person will walk the equivalent of three times around the world.

- The word taxi is spelled the same in English, German, French, Swedish and Portuguese.

- To take an oath, ancient Romans put a hand on their testicles, which is where the word "testimony" comes from.

- Texas possesses three of the Top Ten most populous cities in the U.S. - Houston, Dallas and San Antonio.

- Mississippi has more churches per capita than any other state.

- Portland, Oregon has more strip clubs per capita than any city in the United States

- If you want to email the current Pope, his email address is john_paul_ii@vatican.va.

- 93% of all greeting cards are purchased by women.

- The citrus soda 7-UP was created in 1929; '7' was selected after the original 7-ounce containers and 'UP' for the direction of the bubbles.

- The average person spends 6 months of their life sitting at red lights.

- Most collect calls are made on father's day.

- The first product to have a bar code was Wrigley's gum.

- Average life span of a major league baseball: 7 pitches.

- The first CD pressed in the US was Bruce Springsteen's 'Born in the USA'

- Tom Sawyer was the first novel written on a typewriter.

- 13 people are killed annually by Vending Machine's falling on them. Nearly all while trying to shake merchandise out of them.

- 400-quarter pounders can be made from 1 cow.

- When a Hawaiian woman wears a flower over her left ear, it means she is not available.

- The crack of a whip is actually a tiny sonic boom, since the tip breaks the sound barrier.

- The average woman consumes 6 lbs of lipstick in her lifetime.

- The mask worn by Michael Myers in the original "Halloween" was actually a Captain Kirk mask painted white.

- The average North-American will eat 35,000 cookies during their life span.

- The name of the statuette atop the hood of every Rolls Royce car is The Spirit of Ecstasy.

- Did you know you share your birthday with at least 9 other million people in the world?

- Al Capone's business card said he was a used furniture dealer.

APPENDIX D

Why Can't I Remember Your Name?

You're terrible with names. You forget someone's name within ten seconds of their introduction, and it embarrasses you. In fact, it's possible you won't even approach someone whose name you have forgotten. As a result, you will miss out on a valuable business contact.

If you go out of your way to identify and amplify names, it's easy to show people you appreciate them. A person's name is the difference between a stranger and a friend; the difference between a prospect and a client; and the difference between "that guy," and "Marty, my newest customer."

But in addition to the mastery of these skills, it is equally important to understand *why* you forget them. If you target this problem at its source, you will discover ways to eliminate name forgetting before it begins. You will also become more attune of what stands in your way to make enriching connections with new people.

Attitude

I'm bad with names. I'm can only remember faces. I always forget people. I don't think I'll ever improve my memory for names. I feel guilty when I ask the person to repeat their name again and again.

Change your attitude! You can't continue to make excuses and apologize to people if you forgot their names. If you tell yourself you're terrible with names, you're always going to be terrible – it's a self fulfilling prophecy. Moreover, if you apologize to people, you only remind them that you're terrible!

Focus

I failed to focus on the moment of introduction. I was too busy worrying about the correct handshake. I was overly self conscious about my first impression with the new client. I thought about me and not about them.

Forget about you. Focus on them. This is the foundation of customer loyalty. Smile and make eye contact as soon as they say their name. Repeat it back to them within four seconds.

The Name Itself

I forgot their name because it's complicated. I forgot their name because it's too long. I forgot their name because it's derived from a culture different than my own.

Ask them about the spelling, origin or context of their name. The longer and more unusual a name, the easier it will be to inquire further. As such, this not only allows them to repeat their name, but you appeal to their personal interests. It shows them you care about their personal information, flatters them and makes them feel valued. Usually, they will be glad to tell you about their name.

Memory

I forgot a customer's name within ten seconds of introduction. I drew a complete mental blank. I was humiliated.

This occurs because a person's name is the single context of human memory most apt to be forgotten. Widen other areas of your memory circuit and repeat the name out loud in the beginning, during and at the end of the conversation. When you speak the name, hear the name, and listen to yourself say the name, you will remember it.

Assumption

I assume someone will tell me their name. I assume my coworker will introduce me. I assume names aren't a big deal.

Be the first to ask. Go out of your way to find out people's names. Take your colleague aside and tell them to introduce you to the person clearly and properly. When they do introduce you, be certain to make eye contact with your new associate. This forces you to concentrate on his or her face and name and block out noises and distractions.

Substitution

I accidentally put the wrong names with the wrong people. I confused people's faces. I saw someone's name as an arbitrary fact, and did not turn it into a meaningful representation of them.

Look at people's facial features when they tell you their name. Dramatize those features and make a memorable connection between the person and their name. The crazier the connection, the easier the name will be to remember.

Overload

I was introduced to several customers at the same time. My brain was overloaded. Five names went in one ear and out the other. My memory for names has diffused.

Ask the person who introduced you to quietly repeat everyone's name in your ear. Then, go around the group and say their names to yourself while you look at their faces. Say them over and over again in your head during the conversation. Do this several times. If all else fails, write the names down, look at their business cards, and/or visualize the person's face while you consult your notes.

Practice. Practice. Practice. That's the hard part. But over time you will learn how different methods and tools for name memory will work best for you. Whichever learning style best suits your personality; use any combination of visual, aural or dramatic techniques to remember names.

Attitude. Attitude. Attitude. That's the easy part. As practice enhances your name memory over time, it only takes a few seconds to decide to change your attitude. Don't tell yourself that you can't remember names! Once you have made the decision to go out of your way to remember them, it will only be easier to acquire and master the skill.

Whether you're on a sales call, in the field, work at a conference or serendipitously meet someone again at the grocery store, if you remember someone's name it will be more valuable to you than gold.

You know how it feels when someone goes out of their way to remember your name. That warm sense of appreciation rings in your ear and resonates like a bell down to your heart. It is a pulse of pure human energy. And every time it happens, it brings us closer together. It fulfills our capacity to instantly and effortlessly connect with each other.

APPENDIX E
10 Effective Ways to Remember Names

Sigmund Freud once said "a person's name is the single context of human memory most apt to be forgotten."

Feelings of embarrassment and social ineptitude are conveyed through this forgetfulness, and unfortunately, the problem persists daily. The ability to remember names is an important skill that gives you an advantage in social and business settings. However, the way you associate and remember names is based on your learning style and personality type.

The following list of ten effective ways to remember names combines visual, aural and strategic techniques. Once you find the best fit for you, it will become easier to avoid muttering the most awkward and impersonal sentence in the English language: "Hey you!"

Repetition, Repetition, Repetition

As soon as you hear their name, repeat it back to the person. "It's good to finally meet you, Karen—I hear you're the expert on mufflers."

If you don't do this, you will forget her name within ten seconds of meeting her. Also be sure to repeat the name aloud in the beginning, during and at the end of the conversation. This will allow you to widen various areas of your memory circuit.

"That's a great story Stephanie!" "Wow Tony, you obviously know your hockey." If you speak the name, hear the name, and listen to yourself say the name, you will remember it.

Inquiry

The number one rule in interpersonal communication is to *show a genuine interest in the other person.* So, ask your new colleague to explain the personal significance of his name. Ask if he goes by a nickname. Inquire about the culture from which his name was derived. The spelling question is also effective. Even if Dave or Bob is only spelled one way you can always ask if they prefer "Dave," "David," "Bobby" or "Robert."

In so doing, you show him you care about him as a person. You also transform his name from an arbitrary fact into a representation of him. Ultimately, you will flatter him and make him feel appreciated.

Dramatize Faces

You probably recall faces better than names. Great! This will only make it easier when you dramatize someone's face and associate facial feature with their name. For example, if their nose or hair is particularly memorable, make a connection using alliteration with their name. Brian has bright red hair. Lucy has a long nose.

The trick is to make your associations and dramatizations memorable and interesting. That which is exaggerated and ridiculous is memorable.

Forget About You

"Did I give him the 'cold fish' handshake?" "Did I even look into her eyes?" "Do you think she noticed the logo on my company briefcase?" If you try too hard to make a good first impression, odds are you will have no idea to whom you make a good first impression to!

Don't think about yourself! Forget about you! Concentrate on them. When you become too self-conscious and nervous during the moment of introduction, it will interfere with your memory.

Write Them Down

If you are a visual learner, write down the name of the person. This is a flawless method to remember. Most networking functions and meetings take place where tables, pens and paper are available.

Throughout the conversation, look down at the name in front of you, and then look at the person. Maria. Then look at the name again. Maria. Then look at the person again. Maria. You'll never forget.

The additional benefit when you do this is at least one other person in your group will see you write the name down. Talk about an UNFOR-GETTABLE™ first impression!

Inner Monologue

Imagine you've already used Samantha's name during the conversation. You seem to have it committed to memory. Then again, you don't want to overuse her name aurally. Even if a person's name is the sweetest sound she will ever hear, you don't want to make it too obvious you've used the repetition trick.

Fortunately, there are countless opportunities during the conversation to quickly say the name to yourself while you look at their face: while they get a pen, while they take a drink, while they get something out of their desk, while they laugh at your hilarious joke.

It only takes a few seconds to look at someone and silently think to yourself: "Samantha. Samantha. Samantha." Don't worry; you won't miss anything if you choose to do this at the appropriate times.

Introduce Someone Else

"Have you met my coworker Patty?" you ask the nameless person. "I don't believe I have," he says, "My name is Roger. It's nice to meet you Patty." Roger. That's his name! You thought it was Antonio! Thank God you introduced him to someone else or you would be floating up the eponymous creek.

Furthermore, if you introduce someone you just met to another person, it allows you to: take control of the conversation, show your willingness to encourage connections and expand someone else's network of colleagues.

Listen and Look for Name Freebies

More often than not, you won't be the only person who knows the name of your new colleague. This means other people will say their name, and you will be reminded. No charge. All you have to do is pay attention.

Also keep your eyes open for subtle, visual reminders such as business cards, receipts, nametags, jewelry, table tents and personal papers. Without getting too nosey, it will be easy to identify these "name freebies" that paint you out of your memory corners.

These ten effective techniques to remember names will be helpful to cross the chasm between you and a potential colleague or associate. When you identify and amplify someone's name, you won't suffer a loss of face. Ultimately, your interactions and conversations will become more personal and comfortable.

APPENDIX F
The Nametag Guide

In the past 10 years, more clubs, faith communities, associations, groups and organizations have implemented nametags for their affiliates and guests. And yet, nametags still get a bad rap. People complain they look silly, ruin their clothes, and diminish anonymity.

But for organizations that prepare, create and implement nametags effectively, people will sense the difference. Everyone involved will become more approachable, and therefore better equipped to connect and communicate easily within the group. Ultimately, programs will be more successful because they inspired a sense of hospitality – and not just ANY kind of hospitality: AWESOME hospitality!

I'd like to start this section by addressing several FAQ's about nametags – this time as they relate to organizations.

FAQ: How do organizations implement nametags?

Some organizations have employees, affiliates, guests and other people coming in and out all the time. In order to avoid alienating some of those people, the group must first make a decision: either EVERYBODY wears nametags, or NOBODY wears nametags. (I suggest the former.)

Unfortunately, there will always be people who refuse to wear nametags. The only solution is to make it expressly written externally (signage) or internally (handbook) so people will adhere to the rule. Then, enforce it.

Nobody is "too cool" to wear a nametag.

Another concern is the nametag's potential to segregate people based on position. For example, I am a member of the National Speakers Association. We recently had our National Convention during which each member was assigned a custom nametag based on years of experience, membership or guest status. To my surprise, however, people were actually MORE willing to extend hospitality because of these designations. I couldn't count how many of the veteran speakers who had been in the business longer than I'd been alive came up to me and said, "So Scott, this is your first convention, huh? How do you like it so far?"

That's how you step onto The New Guys' front porch!

On the other hand, if isolation by way of nametagging is a possible threat to your organization, I suggest having the exact same type of nametag worn by all people, regardless of volunteer/member/paid employee status.

FAQ: What information will be placed on your affiliates' nametags?

Other than the person's name, consider including some other personal details such as profession, volunteer job title, employer, hometown, or hobby/talent. This is a great way to expedite networking and break the ice for more engaging conversation. (See the next section for more details on the design of the nametag and placement of information.)

FAQ: What if someone registers late or doesn't have a nametag?

Bring a portable printer, extra nametags, additional lanyards, markers, badge holders and clips. It's always good to be prepared. Also, if a last-minute attendee comes late and needs a nametag, don't give her a second-rate Orphan Tag that looks nothing like the others. She's already embarrassed enough!

FAQ: What is Nametag Deficiency Syndrome?

Over a half of a million people each year suffer from *Emblema Nomenpenia,* more commonly known as **Nametag Deficiency Syndrome (NDS).** This debilitating condition runs rampant through the American business community for many decades, experts say – although only recently was it classified.

Symptoms: You may experience localized font shrinkage, inflammation of the company logo, customer eye irritation due to cluttered texts, absence of upper-chest nametag placement and mild conversational uncertainty and frustration.

Possible Side Effects: Beware of sudden, sever attacks of name-forgetting, possible networking anxiety, unapproachable behavior, missed opportunities to make customers or business contacts, feelings of annoyance due to the inability to say hello to a an employee whose name you can't read because their nametag is turned backwards.

BEST PRACTICES FOR ORGANIZATIONAL NAMETAGGING

Biz Bash,[1] a group of meeting planners in New York, took a survey about nametag preferences, problems and predictions. According to www.bizbash.com, more than 900 event professionals responded within 12 hours and more than 200 responded with comments. Big Badge, a global supplier of nametags and badges to the convention industry co-sponsored the survey.

The biggest nametag peeves among event planners are as follows: waiting in long lines to get your tag, misspelled names, small type size, handwritten tags, using stick-on nametags that ruin clothing, inappropriate use of name tags at unsuitable events, and sloppy execution of last minute attendee badges, making them look like second-class citizens.

- 1 out of 2 event professionals think misspelled names on nametags range from embarrassing to a major problem.

- 1 out of 2 event professionals feel small type size on a nametag ranges from an annoyance to a major problem.

- 3 out of 5 event professionals think waiting in long lines to receive nametags range from an annoyance to a major problem for event organizers.

- 3 out of 5 event professionals feel sloppy execution of last minute attendee badges make them look like second-class citizens.

- 4 out of 5 event professionals feel nametags are unsuitable at black tie events.

- 7 out of 10 event professionals feel handwritten nametags range from an annoyance to a major problem.

- 7 out of 10 event professionals feel adhesive stick-on tags range from an annoyance to a major problem if damage to clothing is a risk.

- 7 out of 10 event professionals feel company names should be present on nametags at business events.

Most Preferred Nametag Style

- Clip-on with Professional Logos
- Magnetic Fasteners
- Lanyards
- Pin-On
- Stick-On

Typeface of Nametags

When asked about the typeface most desired, event professionals chose big, bold letters over sans serif or skinny typefaces. Once again, handwritten tags were considered the least desirable.

Appropriateness of Nametags

When asked when nametags are appropriate, event planners feel they're appropriate at networking events, political functions and at any function in which buyers need to know sellers with the expressed intention of marketing to each other. They felt strongly that name tags are not appropriate at evening cocktail or black tie events.

Reason for Nametags

Most event professionals felt name tags are great for simple identification, while 3 in 10 planners felt name tags can be an important branding tool for an organization.

Perceived Value

When asked about the cost of a nametag, more than half thought the cost of name tags should be less than $1 each, and less than half thought a name tag should cost between $1 and $2.

What Should Appear on the Nametag

Responses to what should appear on the face of the nametag were varied: First name only 4% First name large with full name repeated below and company name the same size 30% First and last name large with company below and without title 38% First and last name large with title and company below 28%

SEVEN DEADLY SINS OF INEFFECTIVE NAMETAGS

Your nametag is your best friend. It is a lifesaver in meetings, trade shows and events to start conversations when you meet groups of new people. It also identifies you as well as your company in the minds of others. As a result, you will become more approachable so you can connect and communicate with anybody. Unfortunately, nametags are useless and ineffective if they are designed and worn without careful consideration.

If you avoid The Seven Deadly Sins of Ineffective Nametags, you will maximize your approachability when you make your nametag more visible, accessible and efficient. You will also discover when you invite people to step onto your front porch, they will cross the chasm between a stranger and a friend, or a prospect and a customer.

Deadly Sin #1: Turnaround

Deadly Sin #2: Size

Deadly Sin #3: Placement

Deadly Sin #4: Clutter

Deadly Sin #5: Presence

Deadly Sin #6: No-Name

Deadly Sin #7: Brightness

HOW TO SPICE UP YOUR ORGANIZATION'S NAMETAGS

What if there was something other than your name to write on your nametag? Obviously, you don't want to steal the show from the one piece of information vital to the success of your nametag. But often, there is enough room on your three inch by four inch plastic tag to add another word or two! The following is a list of several creative things to write on your nametag to empower more interesting and engaging conversations. What's more, it will help you discover CPI's (Common Points of Interest) between you and The New Guys.

Hometown

Casinos popularized this tactic years ago to include cities/countries of origin on nametags to create connections between dealers and patrons. However, any setting in which nametags are worn will engage people to discuss where they grew up. Not only does the nametag promote a conversation about someone's hometown (which shows a genuine interest in the person and appeals to their self-interests), but the self-disclosure reciprocates and expedites the encounter toward a more detailed interaction.

Position

Networking meetings, conventions, jobs or other business gatherings require nametags to identify people with their company or department. But an overlooked addition to your nametag in a business setting is to write what you do, not just your position. Instead of "Oscar Meyer," write "I sell hot dogs to Wal-Mart." I promise everyone at the meeting will come up and say hello! Who knows, maybe they'll want to do business with the person whose nametag made them smile

Pet Peeve

Picture this: you sit down to a table and notice the nametag of the person next to you: "HELLO, my name is Theresa—knuckle cracking drives me crazy." Everyone has a pet peeve, and everyone likes to talk (rant) about it! So next time you go to a casual meeting or event, write your pet peeve underneath your name. You will be certain to have some interesting conversations with this one!

Food

You can always talk about food to spice up the conversation. Include such phrases on your nametag such as "Cereal works for any meal," "Kiwi is the best fruit," and "George likes his chicken spicy." It will automatically open someone else up. They will usually smile and ask about your particular food selection. After you answer, follow up and inquire about their favorite foods as well. This is great for parties and small group meetings.

Nickname

Most people have some sort of nickname they have been called at some point in their lives. And the best part about nicknames: there's always a story behind them. As you discover these fascinating stories, you develop trust, levity and create a friendly bond between two people. After all, if you saw a nametag that said, "Laszlo the King", wouldn't you want to find out the story behind it?

Activities

Write down your favorite sport, pastime or interest. Not only does this allow you to discuss something about which you are passionate, but someone else is bound to enjoy the same activities! Who knows, perhaps you will meet your next teammate or book club member!

Quotation

Write your favorite quotation or motivational saying on your nametag. This is a brilliant method to encourage conversations beyond the small talk level. Many people have some one-liner, old saying, proverb or verse by which they live their lives—so why shouldn't we share them? Wisdom like this is meant to be passed on to other people!

I use this technique during a lot of my speeches for several reasons. First of all, it's fun – it gets the audience interacting with each other. Secondly, it allows people to discuss something significant in their lives. Lastly, it's amazing how much you learn about people when they share a saying or quotation they live by – especially if you live by a similar one!

Entertainment

Include the title of your favorite book, album, movie or magazine on your nametag. Because we learn from every connection you make, this addition to your nametag will be a great opportunity to tell people about some of your favorite things. What's more, everyone saw one movie, read one book or ate at one restaurant you didn't – so use your nametag to spark some future experiences!

Number or Word

Get creative and add a number or word under your name. For example, write the number of children you have, miles traveled to the event or how you know the host. And no matter what the number or word signifies, people will want to find out what it means.

During the wedding of two friends of mine – Brian and Jamie Nogg – the mother of the bride tried this technique with her out of town guests. She instructed each of them to write their relationship to the bride/groom underneath their name.

Throughout the evening, I made note of some of my favorite nametags. First, I saw some of plain and simple references, including:

- M.O.B.—Mother of the Bride
- Bride's Friend
- Cousin of the groom

These simple relationship connections to the bride/groom were easy conversation starters. First, the name of the person was revealed, which was the ticket to starting the conversation. But then, the conversation was expedited when you had a follow up line, for example, "So, you must be the groom's adorable sister Annie."

However, some guests took a more creative role when offering their designated position. And I got the feeling some of these were made up...

- The Un-Groom (Brian's brother, Jeff)
- Brian's Pimp
- Brian's Mother's Father's second wife's sister.

These additions to nametags won't work for every organization, but I encourage you to try it out once. They offer great material for starting conversations and put new and old affiliates at ease.

LEVERAGING NAMETAGS FOR YOUR ORGANIZATION

Here's one final note about organizational nametagging. Last year I published an article in e-Volunteerism, the world's largest Volunteer Journal[2]. It's a resource dedicated to all activities performed by people without monetary profit. The article, Beyond the Mundane, contained a section devoted to using nametags to leverage certain organizational capacities. The following is an excerpt from that article:

Service in the Community. If you are out in the field performing community service, a nametag will be your number one identifier, whether as a volunteer or paid supervisor. It will help the people you are working with get to know you better and quicker. As a result, you will be more approachable to those in need of service and have a stronger sense of connection with those you serve.

Service Learning. Students in experiential education are representatives of the school or institution sponsoring the service-learning, and as such they must be ambassadors. They must represent. Nametags are excellent tools to help students look and act like ambassadors because they hold them accountable for their behavior while they wear it and help maintain consistency between performance and service goals. Like a logo shirt, a nametag personifies a company, agency or school's culture. So teach students to wear nametags proudly!

Pro Bono Work/Donated Professional Services. If you represent a business or professional firm donating its services, don't leave home without your nametag! Although you won't be compensated for your work, your business will still benefit from a promotional perspective. As you offer *pro bono* work, people will make the connection between your nametag and your organization. This will manifest ethical business practices in the minds of the public. And all they'll have to do is look at the logo on your nametag!

Nonprofit Organizations. Most nonprofits are constantly in need of visibility and recognition. Unfortunately, too many nonprofits suffer financially because people don't know who they are! From a marketing standpoint, nametags identify the people wearing them with a specific organization or cause. Think of it as free advertising. So design your nametags in a way that promotes the culture of the group. This will allow you to generate more top-of-mind awareness.